Feckless Cunt

a feminist anthology

Feckless Cunt

a feminist anthology

edited by Susan Rukeyser

world split open press

Joshua Tree, California

Printed in the United States of America.

ISBN-13: 978-0692161746
ISBN: 0692161740

For the women who dare.

Contents

Introduction

It is a word I have used on the show many times, hoping to reclaim it. This time I used it as an insult.

—from Samantha Bee's apology, *Full Frontal,* 6 June 2018

The country was in an uproar: the air was saturated with images of crying children, torn from their mothers and fathers, kept in cages. Stunned parents were paraded for the cameras so we saw them as criminals, less than, other. Trump's "zero-tolerance" immigration policy was a disaster. It seemed a reasonable expectation that his daughter Ivanka, an Assistant to the President who occasionally posed as an advocate for families, might help to clean the mess. But, instead, she posted a shockingly tone-deaf photo of herself with one of her kids wrapped tight in her arms. Samantha Bee called her a feckless cunt.

Suddenly, the cruelty at our border was lost among clutched pearls and shrieks of disingenuous outrage: Samantha Bee said a bad word! The *worst* word.

Cunt—or, as it is whispered by many otherwise mature adults, "the c-word"—is that word you keep in your back pocket. It is the one word you never, ever say…until you do. Then, the shock of *cunt* is a weapon. Forbidden so long, it takes on an almost holy significance.

Cunt is a complicated word because its power is held by those who benefit from gender oppression. There is a reason why the words for female genitalia make us gasp and cringe. Samantha Bee was scolded by some of the same pundits and politicians who helped lower the bar to the dirt for acceptable Presidential behavior. But it was when Donald Trump tweeted that Bee should be fired for her "horrible" language that my brain, fully engorged with rage, burst from my skull and squished down the street in search of a fight. I could not take one more day of it: the hypocrisy. The gleeful hate. The false equivalencies. The violent displays of white supremacy and misogyny. The greed. Trump's smug, petty ignorance. We had all heard him admit to sexual assault, right? Although he said pussy, not cunt. It was not that this moment of hypocrisy and "outrage" was worse than all the others. But it was a moment of ENOUGH.

I posted a call for lean, furious, feminist responses to this moment in the resistance. I gave a tight deadline: July 4, an invitation to declare independence from the petty, patriarchal bullshit. My Inbox became a collective scream.

The fifty-five pieces of poetry and short prose gathered in *Feckless Cunt* offer a powerful, multifaceted response to this one, dumb moment and everything it brought forth in us: how it is to live in our time, in this sexist culture. *Feckless Cunt* is about what we carry and will now set down, what we held off saying but want you to know.

Feckless Cunt opens with the fierce, "Don't Ask Me Now" by Sarah Einstein. She declares:

> When we said *overthrow the patriarchy* we did not mean *vote it out of office* we meant *burn it to the fucking ground.*

We are angry—oh, yes. Because none of this is new. And we are heartbroken. From "What the unfinished self-portrait says" by Brenda Morisse:

> The fucking election is done. When will you
> stop gagging? I know that your map has bled
> to death. When will you stop crying?

Not surprisingly, several contributors directly address *cunt.* Some claim the right to use and redefine the word, taking back its power. Others focus on anatomy, taking ownership of our bodies and our stories, especially the uncomfortable ones: our lifetimes of discrimination, abuse, erasure, shame, critique. But also: rebellion and lust. We're not hiding those stories anymore, either.

> My vagina invites you to a party
> whenever your time frees up
> or now,
> now would be better.

-from Tina Barry's "Party at my Place"

The word *cunt* draws darker work from several contributors. They look at the ever-present, menacing threats that follow girls into adulthood. In "Special Girls" by Alice Kaltman, "Two girls aged eight, free ranging," are approached at a playground by a man who shows them more than they're ready to see, and a glimpse of the women they will be, long after this theft of innocence.

Lisa Allen's poem, "Everything But," thins the membrane between sexist culture and abuse:

> Family night popcorn meant watching
> *Dallas* and *Knots Landing*
>
> meant scratching dad's feet with a fine-toothed
> comb while he rated tits and racks
>
> meant learning smart girls aren't fuckable and
> girls who try to be pretty are
>
> *sluts who think they're too good for the average Joe*

To some, Trump is every aggressive, leering, toxic man who ever treated us like props in the background of his story, toys to be used and broken or laughed at before being dismissed from the room. Several *Feckless Cunt* contributors looked at the silencing of women's stories and complaints and needs.

From Ailey O'Toole's "On Learning Silence":

The first time a man tells me to be quiet before I've even unclenched my jaw, I learn what it means to be a woman and a mouth.

Lately, there is a shift. Surely the 2016 election gave us a nudge. Trump as President was unthinkable, but Hillary Clinton was ambitious, shrewd, insistent—everything women are not supposed to be. Everyone knows: men hate women like that.

Now we see the folly of obeying rules that only serve to uphold the patriarchy. We won't be silent, patient, polite, and oppressed. We're getting comfortable with our anger and our sisterhood and being seen as a little terrifying, maybe. From Susan Abbott's "Nasty Woman Rise: The Dream and The Curse":

Sister nasty woman nightmare hiding under your bed
Sister nasty woman karma gonna mess with your head
Sister boogie-woman karma cuz payback it's time
Sister boogie-woman karma, the pleasure's all mine.

Ultimately, the anthology attempts to reclaim the narrative. From "Taking Tongues" by Sarah Fawn Montgomery:

Today I take tongues
from the mouths of men
like ears soldiers stole
from the dead during wars

There is hope, of course. Without hope, what's the point of resistance? In Kari Nguyen's poignant, allegorical flash fiction, "Rebirth is a Mother," a victim of wartime violence is left to die underground. She imagines a bold escape in which not only her baby, but all children are rescued and held safe by the world's mothers.

In the aftermath of "feckless cunt," these writers say: ENOUGH. We will redefine the language that is used against us. We will tell our secrets. We won't behave ourselves or hush. The pressure built for too long and now our voices erupt like lava—volcanic bombs tearing holes in all the old structures. They can't be stopped or slowed or stuffed back underground.

They will burn you. They will be hot for a long while before they cool.

Susan Rukeyser
Editor, *Feckless Cunt: A Feminist Anthology*

Don't Ask Me Now

Sarah Einstein

We were the young and angry women in t-shirts that read *I Fuck to Come, Not to Conceive* and painted our protest signs in menstrual blood. We shaved our heads but not our pits and insisted on the revolutionary value of our orgasms. When we said *overthrow the patriarchy* we did not mean *vote it out of office* we meant *burn it to the fucking ground.*

So don't ask me now why I'm not clutching my pearls.

I went to a rally after Charlottesville. There, I sang *This Little Light of Mine* with a bunch of clergy and chanted *Black Lives Matter.* The police formed a perimeter between us and those who were there to shout us down. Trouble was expected, but there was none. The counter-protestors seemed disappointed, we were relieved. Somehow, someone from the alt-right found out that I was there, among the hundreds of others, and my name appeared in Reddit threads, Facebook groups, an 8-chan bulletin board. I got calls at work: *are you the Jew Antifa professor who, are you the kike professor who, are you the Feminazi professor who…* My email blew up with death threats: *bash your fat fucking Antifa head in, shoot you in the fucking face, cut off your head and shit down your throat*... Someone sent me a picture of my car at the gas station near my house from an email account that was deleted by the next day. The subject line read: *we know where you are.*

So don't ask me now if I think it's awful that a comedian called Ivanka Trump a feckless cunt.

My litany of the dead is, by necessity, partial because so many of the bodies are hidden. Nonetheless, it's so long that if I began keening it now, I would die before I'd reached the end. Every child shot in school, every refugee refused at the border, every queer who just couldn't take it, every queer bashed for sport, every transperson murdered to preserve the myth of the gender binary, every woman killed by a man who thought she was his property, every woman killed by a man who was angry she wouldn't fuck him, every woman killed by shame at what had been done to her, every woman killed by a lack of access to reproductive healthcare, every person who died of AIDS while the White House still entertained the possibility that it was a *plague from God,* every brown body rotting in prison, every brown body hung from a tree, every brown body murdered by the police.

So don't ask me now if what I mourn is civility.

Instead, tell me where the safehouse maps and the forged passports are hidden. Teach me the codes, the ciphers, and the secret knocks. Give me the key to the secret room in your attic, and help me sew my jewelry into the hem of my coat. The time for asking is over. It's time now to tell, and to do.

Part-Time Patriotism

Keri Withington

He who controls the money
He who controls
He controls
He
He who controls
The money controls
He who controls
The money controls
The government the
Money controls

When you're rich, you can do anything
When you have money, the world is your oyster
slimy expensive

When you're rich, YOU can do anything
When you're rich, they'll beg YOU for more

He grabs them by the
Grabs them
Grabs

NOT MY PUSSY
NOT MY
MY

Can we grab him by the ballot
We grab him by the ballot
Grab the ballot

White women who enable
White women who are able
White women

You are women You are women
You are women You are women

He
He controls
He who controls
He who controls the ballot

Cunt: A Petite Memoir

Donna Jo Thorndale

As power words go, *cunt* remains my all-time personal favorite. My journey to the creme de la creme of power words began in early childhood. Let's be honest, few of us embrace this word casually, nor should we. Ownership and responsibility come with that territory. My first power word, *butthole*, got me a mouth full of Dial soap. I was four. Within a year I was at it again, going for gold with my second power word, *fuck*. My parents were duly impressed with this ratcheting up of the vocabulary and promptly doled out a wicked spanking. Certain words, I was learning, had extraordinary power. Certain words had heft, gravitas, left an impression, got me spanked. As a lover of language, my fate was sealed. I was destined for cursing greatness. Soon, I would embrace the holy grail, the V-8 engine, the honey pot of all power words: *cunt*.

But, why *cunt* as my gold-star standard power word? Ultimately, it's because it is never neutral, never vague, and absolutely, positively, never apologetic. *Cunt* is not followed by a question mark. There is certainty with *cunt*. *Cunt* delivers. Like a laser beam, *cunt* cuts with precision, searing on impact. *Cunt* is powerful and hateful at the same time. And while the intent is usually to insult, its basis is undeniably female. Not only do I *have* a *cunt*, but I can *be* a *cunt*: possessive, vital, engaging. *Cunt* is my blue-ribbon, go-to, Cinderella glass slipper power word. *Cunt* is active. *Cunt* couldn't be passive if she tried. When used by a woman to describe another woman, well, that can be near perfection. So when TV host Samantha Bee hung the "feckless *cunt*" mantle on First Daughter Ivanka Trump, it was active, intentional, and had that Cinderella slipper quality: there was an undeniable, perfect fit.

Ivanka had famously Instagrammed a cuddly picture of one of her offspring while hundreds, if not thousands, of children were forcibly separated from their parents at the Southern border. All this as a result of President Trump's zero tolerance approach to immigrants entering the United States. As her father stood by, blaming Democrats for a policy his Attorney General mouthpieced, Ivanka stayed mum. Oh, the irony. A woman well-versed in branding, who continues to benefit from foreign trademarks and investments under her father's presidency, who claims to work for "bettering the lives of women and children," who has a position in the very White House that is inflicting this trauma, not weighing in on this issue? As a mother? As the First Daughter? "Feckless *cunt*" hit the target. It was the Cinderella slipper. It was the stuff fairytales are made of: magical, breathtaking, mythic, epic.

Marketing Plan

Dori Appel

Ivanka reacts:

Within minutes her ire was erased
by the birth of a brilliant idea. While
feckless cunt still blistered the airwaves,

She planned the ad campaign
for her age-concealing makeup,
Eff-C Little White Lies.

She imagined rows of gleaming bottles
on the shelves of a classy boutique
while shiny ***Eff-C Butt-Kicking Boots***

stomped through the pages of *Vogue.*
The possibilities were endless—
Eff-C **Pillows, Pantaloons, Parkas, Parasols**…

But what about her children?
Wouldn't they be embarrassed by their mother's
trademark, even if it kept them rich

for another hundred years? (And even if
we can't be sure there will *be* a world
a hundred years from now?)

Well, possibly not an *entire* world,
but there will be a really Great America!
Her father is making sure of that.

Daddy's Girl

Gayle Brandeis

My dad loved the word *feckless*
but never used the word *cunt.*
My dad loved the words
pithy and *smarmy* and *bershert*
and *farshtunken* and never
called a woman anything
that would make a woman
cringe. My dad blanched against
language that hurt, language
that stung or diminished,
but I feel confident in saying
he would have no problem
with this daddy's girl
calling that other daddy's girl
a feckless cunt to her
smarmy farshtunken face.

Busted by a Sailor

Tania Hammidi

All depends on the skin /
All depends on the skin you're living in.

—from "Blink Your Eyes" by Sekou Sundiata

In French, feckless means both *Tête sans cervelle* (head without a brain) and *inepte* (inept, to the nth degree). To be without a brain indicates either frivolity or a generous practice of denial, detachment, and failure to navigate social bonds. To be *inepte* (in French), is like being inept (in English), but to much vaster proportions. In French, the word describes the absurd: that which lacks good sense, a lowly place. In this view, to be *inepte* is to consent to one's impotency beyond the imagination, over the edge. In French, the word *inepte* is uttered with vigor and a bit of spit at the end. When there are thousands of real injuries caused by the second kind of *inept*itude, the issue becomes an urgent matter and a collective problem.

Knowing how to place the right curse takes experience, study, and a sense of history. Some say that sailors curse the best; others give that distinction to truckers. Feminism has its legacy of this, too. Word doctors. When Samantha Bee, on her TV show "Full Frontal," busted White House employee/President's daughter Ivanka Trump, calling her a "feckless cunt," my thoughts raced to Valerie Solanas, a playwright with equal parts gutter mouth and quick wit, whose 1967 *SCUM Manifesto* shocked mainstream feminists for its thrashing use of superlatives, and radical feminist stance in relation to patriarchy, and men. Kathy Acker came to mind, full of feminist punk resistance. And I remembered *New Yorker* contributor Kimberly Harrington's knock-knock joke: "Knock, knock? / Who's there? / Ben. / Ben who? / Ben protesting this shit my whole life, feels like."

Samantha Bee risked compromising her professional life and the security of her job to call out Ivanka Trump. This is the edge upon which all good comedy rests. Like a professional, Bee pulled out her best suit to do so: verbal shaming. As a queer performer who has seen many drag queens sling it, I appreciated Bee's excellent delivery and timing. Bee's TV comedy act ignited global visibility, sending a wake-up call to the sleeping daughter, Ivanka Trump, that it was time to rise up. Bee's act bore witness to the thousands of children already "lost" by the bureaucratic US border-patrol system—and yet more still, currently asunder in the routine arms of Republican racism, xenophobia, and militarized government gears, aka Immigration and Customs Enforcement (ICE).

Would Ivanka demand that her father order ICE to stop committing violence against children, mothers, and families crossing the United States border? Could Ivanka recognize the mothers at the borders? See herself in them? Were her ears full of wax?

Feminist activist-academic and abolitionist Angela Davis wrote about language in her 2016 book, *Freedom is a Constant Struggle*. In a discussion about Palestine, Davis creates a spatial image as a way to think about creating social justice movements that are open to many: intersectional. Davis writes, "how to create windows and doors for people who believe in justice to enter and join" the conversation at hand. Comedy often achieves this end, encouraging a mutual place of pleasure, as a way to create shared space. Davis suggests, "So that the question of how to bring movements together is also a question of the kind of language one uses and the consciousness one tries to impart."

With this in mind, a good joke becomes a respite, in language; a plateau to catch one's breath. A place to stand (upon) to navigate the structures and hierarchies which organize society, the media, thoughts, action, cultures, peoples, et al. A place for the brain (whether inside the head, or not). A cervelle (avec têtes, ou pas). A place that can be shared with others.

We were immigrants, too. My father was an immigrant to the United States, in the 1950s. He, along with a team of engineers, helped birth the IBM 1401 and IBM 1620 business data processing machines, among others, onto the planet. These machines were the beginning of the commercial computer created for users outside the military regime (early computing); these machines and their proliferations became the personal computer, from desktop to laptop. My father spoke several languages, including French, English, Spanish, and Arabic. He travelled for IBM business all over the world; my brother, mom, and I held down the house and grew up, together.

While my bro and I were born in the United States, we lived outside the US for our formative years and into adolescence. In Denmark and in France, we developed a communal friendliness to others around us, especially at meal time. I developed my first crush on a long-haired teenager and her friend, while sharing a family-style table at an outdoor café in Paris. My mother's habit of wandering French boulevards with buoyant choreography, from one perch to another, was not easily forgotten by her muscle memory when we migrated back to the United States. She often took us on walks near the ocean, under eucalyptus trees.

This exposure to multitude and many (people, cultures, streets, ideologies, landscapes, languages, desire systems) at a young age prepared me to be versatile and agile, living in the world, now, in the United States. These experiences filled my head (*ma tête*) with diverse sensations, colors, tastes, memories. They made my mind (*ma cervelle*) grow, through consensual experiences and creative engagement. My parents and older brother likely bore many of the initial culture clashes as we adjusted as a family to Southern California. But we were assimilated, visually. We were a white-skinned, mixed-race Arab American family. Our white-skinned lives meant we were not profiled in the ways many Arab-American and other brown-skinned folks were.

It is well known that the United States incarcerates more people than anywhere else on the planet. Since the 1970s, the US has become a nation of mass incarceration. It's a mania of contemporary US culture: to put people in jails and prisons, "away." Not a house full of mirrors, but rather a house without mirrors. Feminist abolitionists suggest that white supremacy, neo-liberalism, misogyny, and advanced capitalism are at the heart of this revolting fact. Proportionally, studies show that 1 in 15 African American men, 1 in 36 Latino men, and a disproportionate number of Asian-American, Pacific Islander, and Native American people are incarcerated, in comparison to 1 in 106 white men. Brown, black, and otherwise not white-skinned people are criminalized, held suspect, and subjected to police surveillance, harassment, and untimely death simply for not having white skin.

And now the US incarcerates brown-skinned immigrants seeking asylum, separating parents from their children. Who wouldn't curse about that? Samantha Bee fully nailed the concept of "feckless" and she cussed like a sailor, as many women do, when they are fed up with all the crap.

In Brief

Liz Abrams-Morley

Used to be haiku—
Poetry's economy
could sing. Now these tweets

bleat. Tweet, twitter, *twat—*
Not to approve that word, you
say, *but when provoked—*

Chickadees in bare
branches, chirp winter hungers.
We hear impending

spring. Perhaps? *One four*
oh characters…and a mule
you quip, fractured his-

story. He fractures
one-forty characters of
Character ass ass-

Ination. Look! I
wrote ass ass, you laugh, and sun
breaks through gathered clouds.

He tweets hate, fear, but
each day holds light later. In
streets, righteous crowds

keep gathering. Keep
laughing irreverently.
Pink cat-eared hats a-

bove which geese blare their re-
turn. From cold dirt—a crocus.
We be resistance.

Song of Our Cells

Kym Cunningham

We discard dreams in bottles overflowing
plastic bins as what could have been
passes thumbtacked eyes slower
than thoughts burn in glass houses
We exchange oranges waiting
for paper laundry while tattooing
no regrets on egos too bruised to see the sun
set on every sad cliché of reptilian temperament
We try not to think
about what lurks amidst the swamp
calling others to drain so
We don't face ourselves
naked and scaled
tearing open capitalism but
knowing faith requires cannibalism so
We cut our teeth on branded
feminism that melts like wonder bread privilege
mothers worried would dapple our thighs
taking ourselves out of context to forget
We were already caught
legally blonde daughters of starched collar
warlords paid to strangle rebellion from
pacifist memories that left

us tasting oil and knowing god is alive but
We are the walking dead
look upon our corp[u]s
ye almighty
and be shook
society demands
We never be stirred
from sleep amidst sounds of gnawing garbage
We try not to call them *people*
trusting children's actors who swing
from exposed condo beams as
We tell innocence
don't look up
keep your eyes trained on your feet
intoxicated by complicity
We believe
survival's an object
best reached on our knees

Made in America

Liz Abrams-Morley

In this home, the fine boned
family china is made to be
smashed, flung against a wall—

Oom- pah!

or tossed into the fireplace,
shards sprayed, legacy shattered.
Splatter the years we saved

to make those down payments,
I say! History
not placed above, on a high shelf,

far from the paws of stray hands
and curious fingers of small
man-children, history

that isn't admired for its
fragile lines, before long
that's at your feet, another need

for a dustpan. Sweep the lore
of the last war, the one before it
into the trash and let's have

another, then raise a Bud! Pour your facts
into cheap plastic cups and pile the used ones up
in landfills. We are the family

who buys all our dishes new
our thoughts at resale shops—
Oom-pah! No worries

says the Pater Familius.
I can always get more where
that one came from.

To the Woman on Facebook Who Called Feminists Angry

Keri Withington

You saved the word *angry* for last
As if it were an insult
Spat out like a bitter thing
Tongue-biting

My 1st reaction is defensive
We are an uprising of love.
But while I type, I realize

I have every right to be angry.

I am angry for my foremothers who wore white
had no right
    to vote were legal property
I am angry because my daughters have a one in five chance
    —Look it up if you want—
    Of being raped in America
    And so do I
I am angry because my son will earn more than my daughters

And while I love him
I know he is no more deserving
I am angry every time I get asked how I balance work and kids
As a judgment not a question
Pre-condemned
And every time my husband isn't asked
As though parenting weren't a joint responsibility
As if men's role ended at conception
And I get treated as less than for either having kids at all
Or for having them and not being home
I am angry because my professional accomplishments have been called
Sad because I'm not home baking cookies
Playing Betty Crocker pin-up
And that the woman who are home
Never measure up either

Let me say it again in case you missed it.
We are an uprising of love.
Feminism is the belief that women are people
And all people are equal and important.

I have every fucking right to be angry.

I'm angry that in America more men named John
Are CEOs than all women combined
And it's 2018
I'm mad that I'm expected to wear makeup, heels,
Suits
My male colleagues wear jeans, band t-shirts

And are still more likely to get promoted
    And it doesn't matter if I work more
    And it doesn't change if I work better
I'm angry that security has to offer to walk
    Me out at night
    Because it's not safe *for a woman*
I'm angry we've never had a president like me.
    And my representatives would rather take bribes
    From lobbyists than *represent*

So no, Facebook friend,
I will not take anger as an insult, even
if it is meant like one. Even if women
aren't supposed to be angry. Especially when
I'm expected to submit.

I'm angry that my lived experience is erased
    By mansplaining, media, executive orders
I'm angry that women are taught to hate themselves
    Hate feminism
That you can't see what feminism has done for you.

I will wear my anger as a badge, bright as any pink
    Knit hat
Because if you're not angry, you're not paying
    attention.

When you say feminists are angry, I say we will
    Harness that anger
    Like a million mills, scorched solar panels
We will burn every vestige to the ground if we
        Have to

We will fertilize the future with this shit
  Women know how to rise from ash
  My great-great-grandmothers worked with less.

Notes from the Pussy Train

Nina Shengold
January 2017

The big Women's March is in Washington, but I don't want to visit the scene of inaugural crime, so I take the Metro-North local down to meet friends in New York. It doesn't occur to me that I'll be riding the Pussy Train.

But it's 8 on a Saturday morning and the parking garage in Poughkeepsie is already FULL. There are long lines of women at every ticket machine. There are a few men *with* women and kids, but this is a pussyhat crowd. The air is full of estrogen.

I walk toward the front with my armload of posters. No seats.

NO. SEATS!

One open seat in the first car. I'll take it.

I scan the rows. One tight-lipped older couple in golf colors. Everyone else is dressed for the march. Petal pink, baby pink, thistle, mauve, raspberry, hot pink, maroon.

We're off! The whole car starts cheering. Noisy group in the back, white women from Rhinebeck, Patagonia vests and determined frizz, starts right in with *Tell me what democracy looks like / This is what democracy looks like.* They're gonna be hoarse by New Hamburg.

I sit back like a salty old pro. My mom dragged her three kids to Moratorium Marches, candlelight vigils and strikes; we were Clean For Gene a decade before we could vote. If there's one thing I know, it's *ya don't blow your voice on the train.* But I can't stop grinning.

One of the Rhinebeck women passes out hand-painted posters. Another walks down the aisle, handing out donuts. "It's my birthday!" she beams. "Can't imagine a better way to celebrate!"

A female conductor comes by, punching tickets, tense jaw. We're an unruly crowd, noisy, jamming the aisles, no better or worse than a trainload of post-game drunk Yankee fans (maybe a little less puking).

Someone yells, "EAGLE!" and points out the window. He's perched on a spar tree, a not-yet-bald juvenile, full-sized and punk-headed in brown like an eagle Ramone.

This is what democracy looks like.

Sun, a white pinpoint burning through haze. Reeds and cattails, curled hands of bare trees.

Pulling into the platform at Beacon. It's *mobbed.* Pink hats and posters, too many to fit. Train rolls in oh-so-slow, and a chant goes up, jubilant:

"Bea-*CON*, Bea-*CON*! BEA-*CON!!!*"

I'm doing the math in my head. This is one train, from one place, heading for a not-main-event march, and it's overflowing. This is going to be *epic.*

A well-dressed black woman sits next to me,

whips out her iPhone and taps, sea-green manicure, brisk. Speaks in accented French, might be Haitian Creole.

Conductor comes through. "Next train right behind!"

Aisles are full of standees. Hiss of a brake release, slow rolling, low mournful horn, three short and one long, like a steampunk barred owl.

White-star sparkles on waves, Hudson Highlands, scar gash of highway through bedrock.

More stops. The conductor gives up. She can't get down the aisle.

Woman next to me calls her boss, tells him in lilting English that she might be late for work, because "There is some kind of march."

I'd love to ask what she does, why her look is so polished on Saturday morning, but it feels too invasive, and she's going to be late for work because all these white women are marching for immigrant rights (among other things), and the bubble we're in just got real.

And outside the window the landscapes are changing from riverfront mansions and boatyards and waterfront parks and West fucking Point sprawling over its cliff to the toxic nuke plant at Indian Point to a hill-clinging trailer surrounded by trash, gravel pits, cranes—the wrong side of the tracks on both sides of the tracks—and the razor wire spirals around Sing Sing prison, industrial rockpiles and spray paint graffiti tags, the American Sugar Refinery, smokestacks and parking garages, a lone urban garden, and all of it, all of it, ratcheting past us too fast to hold onto and *this is what America looks like.*

And our energy pounds down the tracks with that chug-a-chug sparks-on-steel samba. The blue-striped silver cars are called Shoreliners, manufactured by Bombadier, with names lettered onto their sides: Sojourner Truth and Thelonious Monk, Tear of the Clouds and Working Class Hero. We hurtle downriver.

Tell me what America looks like

this is what America looks like

hoo-hooo-hooooo-HOOOOOO on the horn

…and the train slows around the tight curve, Spuyten Duyvil, where my friend Jimmy died when his train jumped its tracks, and every time I round this curve I think of the way his smile crinkled, and somehow there's always a seagull suspended in air, white wings kiting, a sudden hush

RenttheBronx.com, Toure African Market, Jazz Museum of Harlem, flamenco dance mural, Odyssey House: Where Recovery Starts and

this is what America looks like

and the train burrows into its tunnel, the pussy of pussies, and we spill out onto the platform, and every trainload that pours through the doors looks exactly like ours.

And we're swept on a tide of pink into Grand Central Station and onto the vibrating streets where even the cops have on pussyhats and We. Are. Immense. We are righteous and loud and on fire, and *we* are what America looks like

we are what Democracy looks like

and we can never, ever stop doing the work.

Nasty Woman Rise: The Dream and The Curse

Susan Abbott

The Dream

'Twas the night before impeachment
   and all through the land
nasty women were dreaming
    our time was at hand.

Nasty women everywhere asleep in our beds
   while visions of him gone danced in our heads.

The bitches, the sluts, the nasty women cunts
the witches, the healers, all sick of his stunts.
The mothers, the wives, the girls on the side
the sisters, the perverts, the ones he let slide
the crazies, the lezbos, the hairiest queens
the warriors, the homos, the transgender teens
the ones he slipped roofies, the ones that he raped
the daughters he ogled cuz of how they were shaped
the woman he stalked in public debate
the one who had served as Secretary of State.

Nasty the women, nasty our peeps
come to dethrone 45 and his creeps.
The slits, the holes, the tits and the ass
all nasty women—so crude and crass.

Nasty the women oozing juices and blood
nasty the women in t-shirts, wrestling in mud.
Nasty the women, the queers and the crones
say "Enough!" of your guns, your bombs and your
drones.

Our bodies, our selves, the depth of our souls
got our sights on him who's out of control.
Even Miss Universe is down with the plan
to unseat and depose this miserable man

Nasty the women, demons and saints
tired of all his whining complaints.
Dangerous dykes and our sharp battle axes
amazons aplenty demanding his taxes.

Nasty women come to undo this buffoon
get him done gone—it won't be too soon
Nasty women come to halt his Muslim ban
for science and education, we take a stand.

Nasty women rise to save Mother Earth
for all that is holy and brings us to birth.
Nasty women full in labor and strife
speaking our wisdom that water is life.

Strong nasty women he can't bully or flatter
steadfast and insisting, yes, Black Lives Matter!
Nasty women be key to his untimely demise
not sitting idly while the Constitution cries.

Nasty women wild, nasty women free
nasty women bold in our complexity.
Nasty women be firm for democracy's cause
while he makes light of all of its laws.

And while he keeps busy as Putin's cock-holster
his mean ornery ways we never did bolster.
Even as Lady Liberty holds up her flame
nasty women all put an end to his game

Nasty women rise up and be on our way
drain that swamp out of Washington this very day.
Nasty women always fight for what's right
nasty women poised to take back the night.

Nasty women—SCARY!
Nasty women—BOO!
Nasty women be the come-uppance of you!

Sister nasty woman nightmare hiding under your bed
Sister nasty woman karma gonna mess with your head
Sister boogie-woman karma cuz payback it's time
Sister boogie-woman karma, the pleasure's all mine.

So go on and eat all your Kentucky fry
pile on the dairy on that chocolate cream pie
every snot you sneeze, every thing you do
Nasty woman nightmare is coming for you.

Pussy-grabbed Nation just don't give a fuck
cuz that's what happens when you push Lady Luck.
No need to plant bombs, no weapons of steel
you will implode, that news is real.

Come tumbling down, trip all over yourself
your own Trumpty-Dumpty fallen off the shelf.
However it happens, impeach or resign
Nasty Women Nation says, "Get thee behind!"

Now Rachel, now Rosie, now Hillary Clinton
we ain't out of nowhere all us nasty women
On! Barbara Lee! On! Maxine Waters!
Never again let this happen to our daughters
On! Justices Ginsburg and Sotomayor!
Nasty Woman Nation let's show him the door!

The Curse

Be gone, Mr. Trump, we cast our spell
Be gone, Mr. Trump, won't that be swell?
Be gone, Mr. Trump and your Vladimir Putin
Be gone, Mr. Trump, your own horn always tootin'.

Be gone, Mr. Trump, your chaos and tweets
Be gone, Mr. Trump and these Nixon repeats
Be gone, Mr. Trump with your wall at the border
Be gone, Mr. Trump and your narcissistic disorder

Be gone, Mr. Trump and your immigrant purge
Be gone, Mr. Trump and your testosterone surge
Be gone, Mr. Trump, never taking the blame
Be gone, Mr. Trump and your arrogant game

Be gone, Mr. Trump and wherever you roam
Be gone, Mr. Trump, the White House ain't home
Be gone, Mr. Trump, the last and the first
Be gone, Mr. Trump, the nasty women curse!

And so it is!

What the unfinished self-portrait says

Brenda Morisse

The fucking election is done. When will you
stop gagging? I know that your map has bled
to death. When will you stop crying?

Come back to the face of your face. My eyes are
still open and too flustered to blink. Only the dust
mimics your gusts of devotion when you stroked

a cluster of daylight on my cheek, when a tickle
blushed under my chin, when my tin eyes cut
no matter how you indulged me. Now, you refuse

to meet my long memory and salty bust, you smirk
at the bullets in my mouth. You shrug at my
longing and then watch TV—you curse his
blustering muck

and pumpkin face, as he bounces his hairweave all
over the place, his grab and switch groping and
groping and sucking a Tic Tac in lieu of his harried
wet nurse.

I tell you, I would jump out of this canvas and
shake you and your worry. Your light is cloaked in
the nightmare. You're dying with a one thing on
top of another thing headache.

I see your anger huff and puff inside yourself. I
swear you may blow your inmost out if I
were a rotten tomato I'd throw myself at him.

I remind you how my strand of hair teases like a
noose, how my insides are tangled into a strange
quiet. Why don't you recognize the epiphany of
movement

collected in the jaunt of my cap? Why do you hide
my hip under another layer of don't bother me?
Why do you scold me with "Hush. We are
doomed."

Today is the day to direct the traffic of our ululation

Brenda Morisse

Yesterday we cooed to the broken. Last month we prayed. The lucky ones died with hope. The rest of us envy the lucky ones. Let us forget the ground of new character lines and fires, when we shook and still picked up the sticks and looked for survivors. Let us forget the ashes, the wandering ghosts who were promised a heaven. Let us ignore the spirits who pace around the chairs of our memory. The dead who fill out the cloth of our memory and flaunt the shape of our memory. Let us forget them again.

Come! Let us watch the earth fall away from itself. Let us feel the spray as the oceans drop into the sky. Let us find a view worth dying for and eat the windows. Come! Let us swallow light years until we are swallowed up by the light, the fickle light that waited light years to be reinvented.

Let us paint numbers and mathematical functions on our backs. You will be Multiply. I will be Subtract. Infinity is taken. Ha! Let us watch the true division, and addition to the division until nothing is left. Let us argue with zero. Bully it. Negotiate. Let us place our lips upon zero, cover its empty yawn. I hope we are heard. We will not be remembered.

It never occurred to the past that it would be forgotten

Brenda Morisse

That every thorn would need a headstone, every
click a symphony, every tear a jam jar, a hamper of
bloodstained cotton.

Despite my alarm, I cave to the hiss of the
television, the boo and voodoo and boohoo
politics. When will I recognize my cancan, my nude
canvases, the burn

where my halo hit the ground. I rub my face in the
safety of laughter and poke at the generosity in my
closet. Here is my bloom, my milk, the necks of
good returns. The photo where I posed gangster

and flaunting the personality of my middle finger.
Too broke for a loosie, but never too broken to
unfold in silk. When I chose not to crybaby or
make crank calls but to do what I do best—

fall in love. I know how to pick up my pieces and
start again. Even the sky holds its breath until it
turns blue again.

Secrets with Our Bodies

Holly Dunlap

battles lost in all
my hearts, hands, hips, lips

not one cold cut of meat can satiate
the way you do, hands awry on me

the zucchini I used, washed
and ate later

rubbing the back of your shaved head
your t-shirt that reads "Feminist"

soft and wet when I pull it from you
lean on the door, slide, push that

deep place I battle each day, beg my mind
in an open field to dig a trench, stay away

you took my flower with you
I took yours
we both fight these wars

speak a haunting tongue only our own,
speaking of that tongue—

let's have a joust
you can run me through

I Prefer Pussy
(a little city-kitty ditty)

Alexis Rhone Fancher

I prefer pussy, as in cat
as in willow
as in chases a rat
as in raised on a pillow.

I prefer pussy, as in riot
as in foots
as in pussycat doll
as in puss-in-boots

I prefer pussy, as a twat
it is not, nor
is it a beaver,
a clam or a cleaver.

I prefer pussy to
nookie or gash,
it isn't a box,
or a cave or a slash.

I prefer pussy to snapper
or snatch, far better
than taco or
slit or man-catch.

I prefer pussy, though
rosebud's not bad,
and muffin sounds homey,
and cooch makes me glad.

I prefer pussy, as in whip
as in flower,
as into it you slip—
as in *I* have the power.

A Vagina is a Vagina is a Vagina

Hanan Hazime

Would a vagina by any other name still smell as sweet?

lady garden
peach   cherry   flower

flower bud   rose

    kitty   tutu   wee wee   no no   fanny
who hoo   hoo hoo   foo foo   vajayjay

gash   vag
twat

slit   wuss   girly bits

    down there   nether regions

snatch   female privates

cooch coochie cooter cooze   tweeny cookie

muffin

cupcake

jam cookie crumpet whisked biscuit

furry taco tuna taco fur burger bearded clam

cream pie

vadge bone yard

axe wound

tampon tunnel

cum dumpster cock polisher

flange minge quim

poon poontang mossy cleft muff

hot box squeeze box vertical smile
squibbly hole

flytrap

manhole

fagina crotch pocket

cha cha love tunnel

pink fortress crotch cobbler

fetus factory birth cannon

cradle of filth

fun bag

snake pit pin cushion ya-ya

cum sponge tampon tamer

bloody mary love oven cock socket
yoni

velvet glove quivering quim

cod canal sperm harbor

beef curtains meat curtains meat sleeve

hair pie honey pot

bower of bliss

mossy cottage   penis garage   pink canoe

bang hole   coozie   smush mitten

beaver   pussy

platypus   eel skinner

trout basket   panty hamster

semen ashtray   vajizzle

cunt.

Party at my Place

Tina Barry

My vagina invites you to a party
whenever your time frees up
or now,
now would be better.

You see, it remembers the evening
when it left your apartment.
A pack of dogs followed it home.
The neighborhood tomcat,
balls bouncing,
scaled the fire escape,
sprayed the bedroom window.

You wouldn't recognize my vagina now,
it's so well behaved.
Sitting for hours on an office chair,
wearing cotton underpants,
while it yearns for the days
of trimming and perfume.
A walking florist's shop
with the sign swinging.

No need to r.s.v.p.
or bring anything.
Just get here.
The cat's at the window
and dogs circle the block.

The Altos' Garage Sale

Tina Barry

A widow collects her life,
  and the evidence of her spouse's,
    so stacks of flannel shirts

remain, sleeves crossed in contemplation,
  wing-tipped shoes curved with the proof
    of feet. From cartons cobwebbed in corners,

I dislodge gravy-stained linens from meals
  forgotten, tangled wind chimes and their
    melancholy song. Cradled among impossibly

narrow T-shirts, jeans paved with patches:
  my vibrator swaddled
    like a mummified baby.

I recognize it, of course.
  Remember the afternoon in the drug store
    where I spied the flesh-toned package,

an image of a woman on its front,
  device to forehead,
    eyes raised to some benevolent god.

I thought I had entombed the vibrator beneath
photos of old loves. Offered my pre-marital
pleasure to the eager jaws of a trash room
incinerator.

And what pleasure. Each lover exquisite
now in the tumble of memory: pink and white,
olive or cocoa, pillow-haired
and whisky-tongued.

But, *it* gave pleasure too. The motor's early hour
purr, a melody to savor later when meetings
droned and co-workers grated.

For the Altos, I bake buck-a-slice chocolate
pudding cake. Pack water-blemished sheet
music, faux Hermés scarves, a bread machine
that never met a kitchen.

I consider adding the vibrator, too, but no one
would buy a used vibrator at a garage sale.
Even this one that, I discovered this morning,
still hums.

Twat Ghazal

Alison Stone

Lover, tell me what you see down there.
    I tried to look; it's hairy down there.
Jewel of many names — *lotus garden,*
    nappy dugout, muff, yoni, down there.
Long legs, slim hips, but Barbie's missing
    something — just a plastic V down there.
Men's nightmares feature teeth and razor
    blades — a cache of weaponry down there.
Thick books help frustrated women teach
    their men to solve the mystery down there.
If a date cooks dinner, he'll expect
    to dive into the sweet deep sea down there.
Slick magazines are full of vulvas
    and advice: *Don't smell fishy down there.*
Be creative — shave initials
    or a heart. Spread warm honey down there.
Kick him to the curb if he forgets
    your birthday or is lazy down there.
Science says men aren't creeps; nature makes
    them seek variety down there.

Forget my washboard abs and MENSA
    mind. You'll find the best of me down there.
You'll be my true love when you say,
    Alison, I'll spend eternity down there.

Acrostic Love Poem

Susan Abbott

For all the warmth, the depth and resilience
elastic elation and bodacious brilliance
cornucopia of fruits on which I have dined
kin to my kin, kind to my kind
light of my darkness, fire of my freeing
earth of this woman, the mud of our being
solid as space with all its stars reeling
salve for the hurts, whatever needs healing.

Curse not this one, yet let us revere
undo millennia of violence and fear
nourish that power point in you and in me
trust the generous trajectory of our humanity.

Counting the Strokes

Marion Deutsche Cohen

Being a mathematician, albeit one whose big thing isn't counting but who does nonetheless count certain select things like push-ups or scallops on thrift-store candy dishes so you'd think I'd be counting the strokes once or twice in a while but no, it's taken 'til age going-on-75, suddenly here I am counting the strokes and yep, counting and doing at the same time.

19, 20… 49, 50… at our age it goes into the hundreds but yes, it does stop, first because I start feeling slightly guilty about counting, and a tad afraid I'll start concentrating on counting, and then because there are no strokes left to count.

Sex for One

Marion Deutsche Cohen

I am in front of myself with horny-ness.
What I really want is my husband
and he is downstairs.
If I called him he would not do what I'm doing.
He would not spread his fingers in the correct way.
He would not know where my spaces are tonight.
I would have to explain that I like a cloth
between the touched and the touching.
I would have to tell him when to remove the cloth.

Excerpt: Catching Wood

Alzenira Quezada

My clit has been pierced since 1994. I was twenty-four. I couldn't tell you back then if it was an act of youthful rebellion, kink, or mutilation—which was the reputation piercing had back in the day. Friends were popping up with pierced eyebrows, belly buttons, lips, noses, nipples, Prince Alberts—tongues, double piercings, the Monroes—and piercings are still everywhere. We were so gung ho we were punching holes with hollow needles, numbing our skin with ice cubes, entrusting friends with steady hands to perform simple procedures.

Physical pain wasn't particularly a mystery I was ready to explore. I mean sure, I knew about queer play parties where BDSM communities experimented with temporary piercing rituals. I knew that on a socio-political level, that *acts of erotic piercing* were declared illegal in Europe after a group of consenting adult gay men, one of whom is considered the father of modern piercing, were caught in a highly publicized sting, called *Operation Spanner.* But I never thought of piercing as erotic or subversive; even though I was living in the cultural bible belt where it was barely okay to get your ears pierced!

One of my teenage thrills was when mom told me I had *permission* to pierce my ears. She wasn't against women wearing jewelry but she felt earrings were too mature before age sixteen. And that's where it started. A piercing gun at the mall. Eventually, I had three holes in my right earlobe and two in my left.

Modern Primitivism, as it was called in the art scene, was a hot ticket despite warnings from *ABC News* that piercing was a life-threatening epidemic. Body modifiers were considered participants in consensual sadomasochism, but I never really saw it that way. I just pierced what I wanted to pierce—my right nipple, my tongue and finally, my clit. It was more about having authority over my own cunt that prompted me to make the decision.

I got a VCH piercing. It is inserted at the inverted V of the clitoral head. I chose to get a barbell that goes the length of my clitoral shaft. The most common clit piercings are High Ornamental piercing and most folks think a clit piercing means a ring through the head of the clit but that didn't appeal to me.

When interviewing piercers, I was met with a surprisingly misogynistic response from the busiest studio in town. The guy said, *This isn't a gynecologist office... we don't do that shit here... ears, nose, belly button—but that's sick.* The next guy I checked with was a fellow Brazilian brother and offered to grant my request. He measured the length of my shaft with a hollow piece of tubing and remarked that I had a very deep shaft, and the smallest clit he had ever seen. I said, *I know right?*

At the time, I had just learned about female genital mutilation in an article from *Time* magazine. The article hit me in the gut. In some ways I felt like my genitals were mutant, with such a small clitoris and such large labia. Getting off with clitoral stimulation was frustrating and not really my desired way to experience pleasure, but the stories surfacing from these women were hard to comprehend.

Though the crisis was exposed, twenty-nine countries around the world would carry out this crime with help from medical professionals and village practitioners with razor blades, removing both the labia and the clitoris. One of my sisters had a heart-to-heart with me about this issue and I thought about it deeply for weeks as if it were my own story.

I told this to my piercer as he was preparing for the procedure and soon after, he asked if I was ready and there was a slight sting. I felt warm steel become part of my body. It was that quick. It wasn't about kink, it was a personal statement and reason to celebrate what privilege I had been given to have a clit, no matter how small.

When I walked out of the studio there was a kind of a self-satisfaction knowing few would ever know about this piercing. That it would be an intimate secret between me and my lovers. I felt like I had balls of steel hidden in my trousers that somehow validated my masculinity.

My piercing is comfortable and healed quickly

all those years ago, with no repercussions or horror stories to report. It is a constant friend and tickles from time to time to let me know it's there and is ready to work with me. It adds confidence in having a tiny clitoris in a trans masculine female bodied woman.

Most of my other piercings never healed correctly, so slowly I stopped wearing jewelry—including in all the holes in my ears. I never wanted a belly button ring; once contemplated a nose ring after being offered a custom designed ¾ karat yellow diamond, but didn't do it because I wasn't committed to it.

At one point I became leery I was gonna break a tooth biting down on the barbell floating around in my mouth and I took it out. Perhaps a septum ring to celebrate the naughty bull in me (yeah, I'm a Taurus), but then it seemed to me everybody who got pierced, was getting a septum and eventually piercing just wasn't a thing for me anymore. But those hollow holes remain ready to be filled if I so choose. In the end to all my piercings, the clit survives.

Losing My Uterus

Tracy Robert

Before I became a teenager and pulled away from my troubled mother, she told me how much she had wanted me, how long she had waited for me, how many miscarriages she had before she was able to carry me to term. "I prayed for you, Tracy," she said. She meant well, I suppose, but it was a heavy onus to put on a new human. She ended her heart-to-hearts by noting she wanted me so much that she took a drug that "might have been harmful." Those words were a both a clue and a curse.

I heard a biology professor mention diethylstilbestrol—DES—the synthetic estrogen prescribed to pregnant women with histories of miscarriage from the late 1930s to early 70s. US doctors ceased prescribing DES after findings linked it to breast cancer in the prospective mothers who took it, and reproductive tract cancers and anomalies in the children who steeped in it in utero.

When I came home from classes that day, I promptly asked my mother if she had taken DES. She began to cry. "I knew someday you'd find out," she said. "I feel so guilty." I made an appointment for a Pap smear and colposcopy, and I researched the drug—in those days research meant library card catalogs and microfiche readers—discovering that the worst cancer suffered by DES daughters was clear cell vaginal adenocarcinoma. There were stories of women in their twenties who had vaginectomies and vaginal reconstruction because of the rare but virulent cancer, found only in those exposed to diethylstilbestrol.

Reaching my thirties, I crossed clear cell adenocarcinoma off my list of concerns but stayed vigilant about having my annual exam.

En route to my fortieth birthday, however, I had a breakthrough period. This had not occurred in the twenty-seven years I'd menstruated. A Pap revealed questionable tissue. My GP referred me to a specialist, a newly emigrated Australian doctor who took biopsies of what I assumed was my cervix, looked at them under a scope then came back to his lodge-like consultation room (the only things missing were dead animal heads) to discuss his findings. He told me the specimens were abnormal but not cancerous and would need to be watched. I'd come for another round of biopsies in six months.

I must have looked too relieved because then he said, "If you women hadn't been so promiscuous in the sixties, this wouldn't be happening, you know."

I told him I wasn't sure what he meant.

"What I mean is, if you'd read your bible and done what it told you, you wouldn't be having these problems and diseases and such."

"That's not helpful to me right now," I said.

I phoned my GP and asked him to call at his earliest convenience. When he did, I reported my encounter with Crocodile Dundee OB as objectively as I could, adding that I could not work with him. My good doc said, "Completely understood. It's not appropriate for a doctor to proselytize." He referred me to another specialist.

The first revelation the alternate physician made was that Crocodile Doc had taken biopsies from the wrong part of my cervix; they were to have been of the cervical surface and he'd biopsied the endocervix. This new doctor, who'd studied at the University of Aleppo, among other places, took different biopsies, which produced the diagnosis of carcinoma in situ of the cervix.

He left me with a decision to make: have the cancer excised and pelvic exams every four months for the rest of my life, or have an elective hysterectomy, which would remove the cervix, and the threat of cancer. I was the one who first mentioned hysterectomy, not the doctor; in those days the medical industry had rightfully come under fire for performing far too many of the surgeries without sufficient reason.

In situ means "in its original place." The cancer had not traveled. I could spend a couple weeks making up my mind.

I was nearly thirty-nine, separated from my husband, soon to be divorced. Most of my friends already had children. I did not. This did not upset me at all. Moreover, I had never wanted to have children. The term "biological clock" did not resonate with me. Some women spoke of how they loved or reveled in being pregnant, but it held no appeal for me. The nausea, the threat of preeclampsia, the swelling of the body like a melon ready to split, the pain and mess of delivery—this all sounded more than vaguely horrifying to me. One of my friends told me her pubic bone cracked during the birth of her second son. I couldn't imagine the agony of that, coupled with labor contractions, and seriously wondered how our species propagated as long as it had.

Apart from the pain of pregnancy, I balked at the dubious outcome of it. Parents were responsible for the beings they produced at least eighteen years after bringing them into the world. I'd been teaching high school for over a decade and had seen the optimal and worst results of procreation, and I'm not talking about intelligence so much as character. When I thanked parents for their conscientious and cooperative kids, some of them remarked that they weren't sure how they turned out so well. When forced to contact parents about student behavior problems, I heard from many of them that they'd tried all sorts of strategies, none of which worked, and were at a loss for what to do next. They asked me, a childless woman, for ideas. I empathized with these parents because I too had tried different strategies with their kids, but I drove away from the school and the problem students at the end of my work day, and the parents left work and drove to the homes in which the culprits, the fruit of their loins, lived.

Nothing about childbearing beckoned me.

A good and caring friend, who'd given birth to her first child at age forty, appealed to me to have my eggs harvested and frozen, in case I changed my mind about being a mother.

"What for?" I said. "So I can pass this DES crud along to someone else?"

She worried I was making decisions out of fear. All I could envision was the expense and discomfort of egg retrieval, and these tiny larval bits of me languishing for years in a laboratory freezer until I came to my senses and had them destroyed.

Before my surgery, I signed a form allowing Dr. Aleppo to use his judgment in determining whether my ovaries presented a health threat sufficient to require removal.

My sister told me the surgery took over four hours and my ovaries were gone. Endometriosis, a form of abnormal uterine tissue, raged through my entire pelvic region all the way up my fallopian tubes and covered my ovaries, which were riddled with cysts, some of them burst. When Dr. Aleppo visited my room on his rounds, he said, "It was a junkyard in there. I cannot believe you walked upright."

That explained the cramps I experienced every month, so horrible they shot spasms down my legs. Twenty years after my surgery I'd discover DES daughters are 80% more likely to suffer endometriosis.

Upon my return to work after six weeks of leave, a feckless, antediluvian boss asked me how I was dealing with "no longer being a woman." I honestly laughed out loud at his question and said, "I'm pretty sure a uterus and ovaries aren't what makes me a woman." He cringed at my direct mention of lady parts and the conversation ended.

Nonetheless, I pondered his remark long after he made it, and the swiftness with which I responded. I felt more like a woman post-surgery than I had before, because I had seen myself through a harrowing journey, one that began with my mother's clue/curse when I was a child. When the curse arrived on my doorstep, I encountered a charlatan offering assistance and rebuked him. I trusted my own mind. I came out on the other side a survivor.

If survival doesn't make me a woman, what does?

Supporting Actress

Devon Oretga

"What is my role?" I say.

— You are the lynch pin, the glue so to speak. Also, you cook.

"But," I say, looking at the script, "where does it say that?"

— Let us worry about that. Now, ACTION!

"But what's my motivation?"

— ACTION! ACTION!

(I don't know my lines. I choke. I bumble scene after scene.)

"I don't even know what character I am!" I bemoan to others backstage while juggling things I am handed.

— Lots of people would kill for your part. Absolutely kill. (Several of them make slashing gestures. One mimes choking an invisible rival.)

Shuffle onstage

"I'm in love!" I say to the back wall of the theatre. There's applause behind me.

— She's sure as hell not winning any Oscars again this year!

"I'm trying," I call out to the spotlights. "I want to do better. I'm trying!"

Dance

— Can someone show her how to dance harder?

(Keep going until someone calls cut.)

Second Person

Caryn Davidson

Why can't you surprise me sometimes?
Slip a chocolate tulip into my purple lunch bag,
or hide an Indian paintbrush in our bed.
Why don't you ever delight me with
an unexpected lupine in the toothbrush cup,
trip me up with a note, written in blood,
left carelessly on the granite counter?
A chip of obsidian glints in the pale, gritty sand.
The impassive face of a spiny lizard greets me
as I round the corner on the oasis trail.
Claret cup blossoms pop from the drab background
of invasive grass and forbs, quickening
my awareness, yet, you do no such thing.
Why can't you disarm me sometimes,
hang a curtain of wild hyacinths across
the threshold of our morning habits?
Encircle me with your embrace and dance me out
to the porch, make a headdress fashioned from
quail feathers and flecks of quartz, or
surreptitiously add, "Don't forget the jimson
weed!" to my weekly shopping list. Why
won't you surprise me? Make me wonder
who buried the seashell in the sugar jar,

how the painted lady landed in the butter dish,
when the living room clock sprouted violet phlox?
It might be high time for me to
fold this poem into an origami swan,
and place it in the cocoa-colored fleece you wore
the night we dragged the mattress under the stars
during a conjunction, when Venus shone so brightly
at the moon.

Glutton

Sarah Fawn Montgomery

We learned the sin of satisfaction—
our mothers and theirs growing
large each day, widening like the moon
we turned our faces toward each night,
hung in the darkness like a beacon.
Over years of hollowness—hearts
and bird bones—the women grew full
on regret and Diet Coke, sucking
at their only bit of sweetness
day after day until their faces shone
round. *Glutton*, folks spat
when they had to move around
sashaying hips, or when the last roll
was claimed from the breadbasket,
butter glistening on succulent lips.
And though our mothers and theirs
warned us against this legacy,
rans hands along the lengths
of our spines, a gold star for each
vertebra, or praised hunger,
the way our hipbones protested,

this was eclipsed when they pulled us
like the tides to their laps,
their bodies celestial and gigantic.

Your Mother Knows

Holly Dunlap

She made a path out of herself for you.
You turned her inside out, and she survived.

You're her cells, her twist and ladder.
You came in on a wave of red, a soft carpet.

But you call me, "artist crazy, but the bad kind."
You forget her face, her tired eyes and feet.

Your face is smooth, careless, and you travel alone.
Airport to airport, train to train.

Maybe she taught you to move between words, but
I doubt it, and you took me,
ignored me, stripped me of nutrients,
my willing hands, and walked away.

Crazy, hysterical vagina, my mouth,
places for your penis, holes,

like the one from which you
emerged, wet and helpless.

My brain, my heart, my disembodied hands:
Organs and appendages, worth little to you, boy, but

my vagina's a poet, a port to wisdom
you will never have,
and your mother, like myself, bled for you.

The old woman is pissed off (again)

Judith Arcana

because (again) her actual self has been
denied—with a smile (of course), denial
offered as a favor, a kindness, a sweetness—
the speaker assuming she'll be flattered
to hear that who she is, the old woman
what she is, an old woman, is not really
(not now, not here) who or what she is.

"Oh no! Not even close!" says the cashier
when the old woman asks for the elder
discount on her grocery bill. The cashier
smiles as those words slap the old woman
sliding her credit card along the sensitive
rim of the register computer that will
(or will not) approve of her.

They always smile when they do this.
She can see what they expect: she will
accept denial, take erasure as the gift
they mean it to be. They're giving her
a gift, saving her from the awfulness
of her own true life, and they want her

to smile about it, join up and pretend
(makeup, hair dye, cosmetic surgery)
—pretend she's not who she really is:
a woman, grown old, out in the world
buying radishes, cereal, soap, cookies.

To the shitty white hipster boy who didn't understand why I sent him a screenshot of the Wikipedia page for manic pixie dream girl, but instead managed to make the conversation about himself, yet again

Ailey O'Toole

I did not mean to imply you were a "broodingly soulful young man." I meant that I feel like you treat me like an ornament in your house, only here to further your own story, rather than recognizing I am a forest fire that has already been lit, that I exist outside of you, that I am too big for your house and there is no making me smaller. Everyone has darkness inside them and I do not occur merely to show you the exit to yours, especially when I am still searching for an escape from the parts of myself that the light doesn't reach. I will not be your radiator. I am not here to introduce you to what it's like to be warm. I am a stick of dynamite and I am not asking you to strike the match. You cannot squeeze me into an inconceivably small corset so you can feel bigger than me. I prevail outside of your depression and I do not want to be made to fit into it with you. My sisters and I, we are humongous. We are rainforests sprawling across continents, oceans holding hands across planets. I do not want to live in your house when I have my own damn home that I built with my two good hands, hands forged in the histories of Artemis and Aphrodite and Athena. You cannot mold me like clay so that I fit into how you see the world. I am the stone that Michelangelo carved, I am the lioness prowling the Sahara, I exist in my own habitat that is far greater than anything you've ever built. I have no interest in fitting into your story when I can live in the rest of the world. I exist outside of your sad narrative and I swear to the goddesses, if you try to make me into "that bubbly, shallow cinematic creature" that I was trying to make you aware of, I will explode and take you down with me. I exist. Let me exist.

Benediction From The Muse

Genevieve Kersten

i come when called
wipe dribble from your mouth

we both know you can't create
without mother-helpmate-servant

i watch you write a poem
then set it on fire again

you claim this pays tribute to me
but you only serve yourself

your wet breath repels me
i gag on your tongue

you rant about my fickle nature
then refuse to see me sober

i tire of your hangovers
and thick smoker's cough

you chisel my patience
i'm loosed from stoned servitude

and now the closing of thighs
parting of ways

this is the last i will know
yellow-stained fingers

i seek a vessel
not a leech

here is my final gift to you—abandonment
let it serve as inspiration

Learning from the Male Artist

Devon Ortega

I told him my favorite poet and he cackled,
"You must be joking!" and then I think he puked
or maybe made a puking sound? It's a shame
I can't remember right, my memory's so tainted.
He didn't like my writing because it was
undignified, vulgar—all the words just thrown,
like so much unwarranted telling. He said if one
uses a thesaurus they don't belong
in poetry. And he was right. I used a thesaurus
because I wasn't sure the words
I wanted existed. The feelings I had
were slippery and hard to grasp; I looked them up,
ashamed of my lacking vocabulary.
But I just wanted to speak!
"How tacky," he'd say, and then systematically name
all of the elements I was, and always would be, out of.
I was so crass in my writing and ostentatious,
writing about bodies and infidelity.
He discounted each poem to the bargain bin,
big, garish stickers that said -2 cents.
I used the word *pecker* once and he laughed at me.
Continued laughing for hours, ha ha-ing while
his eyes wildly darted from face to face,

desperate for everyone else to laugh with him,
and eventually they all did, even me,
because it's obviously called something else, stupid.
We were just so different, him with his not-pecker
and me with whatever women have.
His mysterious, light-touch poems and mine
with their weird line breaks and large breasts.
We just couldn't coexist because he showed
the world itself and I just grossed it up
with my lack of culture. Because
I never wrote about how a swan looks
floating, placid on a lake—because I know
underneath the still water
he is shitting shitting shitting
on everything below.

When Barbie Bleeds

Ann Marie Gamble

Don't go boy-crazy easier to be a boy
Throw out the curling iron eyelash crimper lip
        plumper stomach binder
Skirts too high too tight too long too loose
Show some confidence just not here don't
        touch not after dark
A heel is a person who acts like these shoes feel
Climb a tree talk back let someone else
        bring the cake
I'm sorry I can do the math at least
        78 percent of it
Smile when you tell me that's your space your
        time your reason to succeed
Otherwise whose girl are you?

Important Research at the Telephone Survey Center

Genevieve Kersten

My phone voice is a solid octave
above my regular voice.

It creates a whole different person,
one who listens when you talk.

She giggles and titters in response
to your clever remarks.

She even awws all over you
if you've had a bad day.

Her days are never bad,
not compared to yours at least.

She fawns and simpers
and you answer all her questions.

Including the ones about your last colonoscopy
and whether or not you feel like a failure.

When the survey is completed
you thank her.

She knows you will masturbate
to aprons and pot roasts for a week.

At shift's end there is a brief exchange
between my voices, phony and real.

Awkward shuffle of mental papers,
gathering of imaginary belongings.

As she steps aside her close-lipped smile
an implicit offer to take over full-time.

On Learning Silence

Ailey O'Toole

The first time a man tells me to be quiet before I've even unclenched my jaw, I learn what it means to be a woman and a mouth. All my edges are too big, need to sand down the parts of myself that aren't pretty, learn to fit into this lifestyle of pink razors and mascara and wordlessness. I pull my knees against my chest, squeeze them tight, wonder if I stay still long enough, will I learn how to be smaller?

The first time a man I love tells me to just keep my thoughts to myself, I practice curling my tongue in my mouth, consider how strong it would have to be to say something that caught his attention, made his breath stop in his throat. As I practice being silent, "more palatable" as my mother says, I rehearse all my thoughts in a voice I don't recognize, ponder running away and remaking myself, painting my lips the bright red color my father says isn't "ladylike." I think of all the things I could do if women were allowed to live how they wanted. I would do them all.

If I could, I would never stop talking. I would tell the world that being a woman means no fear of blood, means housing a whole lot more strength in your body than a man ever has to, means having a heart not the size of a fist but the breadth and gravity of a tidal wave. I would tell every girl under thirteen that magazines are wrong, men are wrong, their mothers are wrong. It's okay to have thoughts that slice men's flesh, it's okay to be loud and unwavering, it's okay to be a woman and a mouth.

Spreading My Legs for Someone (Posing for Pirelli)

Alexis Rhone Fancher

The grey-suited Pirelli rep. sat behind the desk,
puffing on a cigarette. White smoke hung in the air
like surrender.

I slipped off my dress.
Kept my stilettos.

There was nothing on the agency man's glass-topped
brain but my nakedness.
He wouldn't meet my eye.

"Jesus!" he exclaimed when I bent over
to tighten an ankle strap.

The photographer looked like Antonio Banderas.
"Sit down on the seamless," he said, pointing to the
black backdrop that spilled onto the floor.

He rolled the tire over to me, snapped on the lights.
I sat, cross-legged, clutching the tire close.

My naked breasts peeked through the center,
the nipples erect. I laid my hot face along the tread.

The photographer pushed up his cashmere sleeves,
picked up his Nikon.

The lights bore down like August; the cement
below the seamless bruised my ass. The two men
stared at me the way my stepfather did.

I pushed the damp strands of hair from my forehead.
Arched my back. Opened my thighs.

The suit lit another cigarette.
Antonio Banderas moved in for a close-up.

"Is this what you want?" I asked.

My feet poked out from the tire's rubber frame
like destiny.

Mirror

Caryn Davidson

Not yet in place was
That diabolical mechanism
As I sat naked, six years old, my legs apart
Before the mirror,
Exposing parts that otherwise I could not see.
I was curious and not much more than that,
    When Oma walked into the room,
    then turned and marched
    with solemn, outraged steps to
    Tell my mother what *she* saw.

    At that instant I was initiated,
    Plunged into that first confounding freeze
        of shame,
    Seared by the acid fear that immediately
        invades the body.

The ceremony dictates that you braid one strand of
        terror,
One dark hank of cold humiliation, and a thread of
Speechless indignation.
Next the braid is lowered down the throat but do
        not choke

For this is the conductor for the jolt,
The charge to galvanize the focus,
Shift all time and shout:
I am revealed and
Am no longer merely me and naked, six years old, my legs
Spread wide apart
Before the mirror,
Exposing parts that otherwise I could not see.

Special Girls

Alice Kaltman

Jessica and I wandered around the empty playground on a dim Saturday morning. The late autumn air was ripe with moldy overtones. A dull grey sky spat on us. Two girls aged eight, free ranging. Her house was around the corner, out of view. Were her parents even home? Back then it made no difference. Kids roamed freely. Parents hoped they didn't do anything too stupid.

True winter was a month away, but already everything was shut down, hushed. The tether balls were off the poles, the volleyball nets gone. There was cat poop half-buried in the unattended sandbox. Other kids were inside watching Saturday morning cartoons on bulbous black and white TV screens, readjusting rabbit ear antennas to quiet the static hiss or fix the fuzzy lines of colorless robots, silly bald men, hyper-active coyotes. Other kids were warm. Other kids knew better.

We decided on the swings.

I'd forgotten my mittens, so I kept my hands fisted and shoved up my sleeves. I hugged the metal chains with my elbows which made for very aborted, unsatisfying rides. The bracing wind found any exposed spot it could to torture me; my cheeks, my ears, the space between my anklet socks and my stretch pants. Each turn of my head reminded me of the dangers of zipping my parka up too quickly. I had a red and raw spot just south of my Adam's apple that wouldn't stop throbbing, as much as I tried to ignore it.

Jessica seemed unfazed by the foul weather. She swooped next to me singing, "Alice Alice Bo Balice, Banana Fana Fo Falice, Me My Mo Malice…Alice." To this day, whenever I hear that inane ditty I become eight year old Alice again, awash in dread.

It had been Jessica's idea to go to the playground in the first place. Jessica was a new and exotic friend, a restless dark haired beauty with two sisters in high school and parents who were bona fide communists, or maybe just college professors. Jessica, like me, was a youngest. We were both "surprises" raised with benign neglect by parents who were old, who coddled or ignored us, depending on their energy levels. Often we were allowed to do just about anything we wanted. Fun stuff. Stupid stuff. Perilous stuff.

I saw him first. A pudgy man in a trench coat with skin the color of unbaked bread. Everything soft, unassuming. Poke-able like the Pillsbury Dough Boy. He raised a hand and weakly called "Hi girls" as if he knew us already. When he got close enough I could tell the difference between the spitting rain and the beads of sweat coating his forehead.

Jessica wasn't paying attention, so enamored of her own voice.

"I'm John," he said to me as I swung in tepid arcs. "I'm a friend of your mommy's."

Don't Talk to Strangers. That was as far as the warning got back then.

A friend of your mommy's. I didn't call my mother Mommy.

Jessica, on the other hand, would shine in any spotlight directed her way. She noticed "John" and stopped swinging, her stick-skinny legs in polka dot tights dangled towards the ground, her patent leather Mary Janes skimming the sand like tassels.

When Jessica smiled at John, I could swear I saw him shiver.

"You girls want to see some silly postcards? I have them here in my pocket. They're really funny."

Silly. Funny. My heart fwump-fwumped deep underneath the sticky zippered parka, my itchy wool sweater and flimsy Carter's undershirt.

"Come on. Get off the swings and we can go over there—" he pointed to a wooded area of the park. "I only want to show them to you. I don't want other kids to see them. Only kids I know. Only special girls like you two."

Jessica looked at me, her eyebrows raised in a what do you think, sounds fun to me sort of way, and in that moment I realized; as much as Jessica would always be an object of desire, and I would envy her that for many years, I would always be the voice of reason, and she would envy me that forever.

But I was only eight, and so not yet as reasonable as I would ultimately become. Pleasing a friend. Seeing funny pictures. Maybe John was a friend of my mother's after all.

We followed John to the woods. We saw the postcards. He flipped through them slowly, breathing heavily, watching us look. Mounds of flesh in positions we didn't understand, limbs and body parts and murky, dark patches of hair.

I had no idea what I was looking at but still guilty shame seeped into my pores from the first glimpse of shoddily photographed flesh to the last. Jessica seemed fine. But what did I know? Maybe her cheeriness was already part of her facade.

"Do you girls want to come with me to my house and see more?" he asked us when we'd seen them all.

It was a good thing I was a mistrustful kid by nature. It was a good thing Jessica was basically a follower.

I saw John a few months later at the local toy store. He smiled at me as I clung to my mother's hand like a lifeline. I don't think he recognized me because he looked away, back to restocking Chatty Cathy dolls. A new employee, he smiled at everyone. He smiled at the next kid. And the next. And the next.

Everything But

Lisa Allen

Family night popcorn meant watching
Dallas and *Knots Landing*

meant scratching dad's feet with a fine-toothed
comb while he rated tits and racks

    meant learning smart girls aren't fuckable and
girls who try to be pretty are

sluts who think they're too good for the average Joe

            meant sitting cross-legged
            on the floor in front of his recliner
            silently
            cataloging which muff
            he'd like to dive and
            which actress he'd bend over the desk to

fuck the shit out of
                meant learning girls who say **no** are

dumb bitches who don't know what's good for them

meant feeling cheeks pink when he said *beaver*
and I thought he

meant the creature

meant learning men want tight
twats and bouncy boobs

meant hearing girl's mouths are

meant for one job only

meant thinking the space

between my legs
was square and
folded in upon itself
if assembled right

meant knowing men are only men
when they
give it to her good
and girls are only good when they

take it
meant never wanting kids
because giving birth
stretches that shit out

meant not trusting the guy who just
wants to get in your pants and
knowing

they all want to get in your pants

meant sawing that comb between his toes
until
his skin broke

meant listening to him groan

yeah yeah yeah harder

meant being dateless through most of high
school

meant bowing my head in hopeless surrender

meant remembering the magazines I sneaked into
his room to see

meant the shame in my panties when I looked at
the pictures and the point of my nipples when I
read *Penthouse Letters*

meant

steeping in stereotypes and expectations and
returning
to the floor in front of his recliner when
I look at myself in the mirror now
reduce myself to parts

means wondering if daddy's little girl ever grew
up

means still wanting to please, be pleasing, pleas
to stop please stop

means realizing dad is Donny and Donny is
dad, uncle, cousin, friend, teacher, preacher,
good guy, that guy—

—feeble men wielding power like
bloated sprinkler hoses
jerking on the lawn
useless but for the swamp
left in their wake

C for Chris

Janette Schafer

What I remember about Chris now, thirty-three years later, is the dark blonde bowl haircut, perpetually dirty fingernails, and slight snarl of the lip.

We sat next to each other in sixth grade math class due to an unfortunate accident of alphabetical order by last name. On the first day of class, he leaned over as the teacher wrote on the blackboard and bit my ear, snorted like a pig, and told me I was disgusting. A few days later, he reached under the wooden desk we shared and grabbed my vagina, squeezing so tightly that I almost cried out except I did not want anyone to know what was happening. When he failed to get the response he wanted, he gave me a sharp poke in my tender flesh with a #2 pencil. Tears and a sharp intake of breath; otherwise, no sound.

He slid a note to me saying he wanted me to write down what he had done so he could show his friends. He promised he would stop if I wrote it down. So I wrote it down.

After, boys sniggered and slammed into me as we passed in the hallways. One day sitting near The

Beautiful Melissa in science class, she turned and whispered to me, *Everyone knows that you're a whore.*

I was different after that. For weeks, I prayed as I fell asleep to not wake up.

As for Chris, he lied. He did not stop.

I never told my parents what happened. This is the first I have ever written of it since the note I gave him that said, just as he had dictated: *Chris touched my cunt with his hand and his pencil.*

She/Me

Jana Martin

Cunt, feckless and reckless and guileless and blameless and intentionally positioned to aggravate all the fear-boys and toothed or grooved or magical or poisonous or toxic or gravitational a black hole of possession of control of mood swings of needs, so many needs, fill me, drill me, will me, kill me. I have been a cunt since so young, a godfather turned me from girl to aware, said *do you know what a cunt is*? I was aware in a confusing, dirty way, looking in the mirror and seeing me as this complicated budding column of flesh with a warm hole, this tease in a bathrobe. He said *You're only eight and already such a tease* and me not knowing why, how was I a tease, how a person how a girl how anyone could be a tease and what was I teasing I wasn't teasing, but soon knowing there was a reason the boys wanted her/me that wasn't her/me, that wasn't what she said that was just between her/my legs the pronouns wildly churning *is it me it is her is it me is it she*

go bother her she probably would like it more is what I said in a terrible ineffective ten-year-old's voice to that older boy or young man I could never describe him accurately enough on Madison Avenue who came up behind me, broad daylight, grabbed the hood of my orange sweatshirt slipped his hand down the side of my overalls because I was until a month before a small town girl, a country girl, a cuntry girl see how that works so innocent 'til when he said *pretend you're my wife pretend we're married see how I walk with my wife* and he said *let me touch your pussy my wife* and on Madison Avenue in 1973 it might as well have been cunt to all those upstanding folk trying to avert their eyes and not look at those two walking with his hand down her overalls. Then for a year I made frantic drawings of violations factories of violations rooms of mass violations, the she not me the her not me them them them and in a way it was them, I hadn't even gotten my period yet and the handsome shrink who wore ironed blue jeans and adidas in his immaculate dark office said *Well, are you angry* and I knew, I knew you're not supposed to be angry at grownups at adults at me and be polite and be sweet so I said *Not really*, a lie as deep as the pile of drawings hidden under my bed a lie as deep as the tunnel into the center of my body

years later in womanhood anytime someone said *hey baby hey pussy nice pussy* I'd shudder go numb then want to kill them quietly, silently, internally, there is energy in rage and so it would come out, a flash, a rush a frantic detangle out of someone's arms and racing down to the subway to get into a long anonymous train and ride out into the dark and then someone said how can you be so scary pussies aren't supposed to be scary and I knew what he meant, pussies, aka girls, aka cunts they're supposed to be soft and things you go into but I kept thinking of all that negative space inside me, violated and disturbed and quiet and dark, waiting until the right moment, waiting.

Thank goodness for my sake for the sake of orgasms and melting desire and that moist throb that is a girl's best friend thank goodness I found other ways to enjoy it, *just don't say cunt, please don't say pussy* and so on the surface on my skin it went away, not the aversion to the words but the aversion to aversion and I went from she to me, saw myself through my eyes not theirs and I understood my own pleasure, I wanted it hard and clear and unequivocally to be about me not a body part not a generic she not a hole.

But sometimes the wisdom of a newly cynical girl and the seep of old violation came back again and it was either give in or escape all over again and depending on whether I felt like a pussy or a cunt I did. And then there was a new division: a pussy is a victim a cunt is something, something else. But at a certain age your genitals become your very being, you graduate from having a cunt to being a cunt, and that is another violation just as sudden just as abrupt, just as many people watching you on Madison Avenue turning into that very thing, what a cunt, *she's so angry*. Of course I'm angry. But I'm not feckless, I really have plenty of feck so be careful, watch the feck, I might spread my legs and kill you with all my feck and I know and you know you'll deserve it.

On the Argument that Men Should Not Be Prevented From Getting Jobs In Their Field After Being Fired For Workplace Sexual Assault

Ailey O'Toole

My best friend tells me Kevin Spacey
shouldn't be prevented from ever working
as an actor again just because he raped
that boy that one time and suddenly I am
14 again and my high school soccer coach
who is also my biology teacher is inviting me
back to his house after the tournament,
sliding his hand up the small of my back
as he tells me he has plenty of beer and
"Maybe we could have a good time together."
I do not know how to tell him no.

My mom tells me that just because a professor
is fired for sexually assaulting a student doesn't
mean he should have his livelihood taken away
even if it was an abuse of power and suddenly I
am 18 again and my chemistry TA has me pinned
to a park bench, slamming himself inside of my soft
pink flesh and I can feel the bruises rising on my
back but I don't tell him to stop because I know

I'm not supposed to. I know that because I told him I wanted it at one point that I have to let him have this, even if it's hurting me.

JK Rowling releases a statement about hiring Johnny Depp for her new movie despite his wife's allegations of domestic violence and suddenly I am 20 again and my manager is grabbing my ass every chance he gets, telling me how badly he wants me and there are those words again: "Maybe we could have a good time together." Even as he presses his erection against my thigh, I know that saying no will at least cost me my job, if not a flurry of physical attacks because haven't you heard about all the girls who have been killed for saying no?

What am I supposed to do when a man who has power over me demands I give my body over him? How do I say no to these men when doing so means risking everything I've built?
Don't you dare tell me that these men deserve to keep their jobs, to remain in positions of power, to continue being paid while taking advantage of women who can't say no. Not when those men are taking away my right to my own body.
Don't you dare tell me that they shouldn't be stripped of their livelihood after they've stripped me of my ability to ever feel safe, to ever trust a man, to ever be able to have sex without worrying about how I will ever be able to say "stop."

I am almost 23 now. I have learned that saying no is not easy. But I have also learned to scream. No one can take that from me.

Halloween

Eva Schlesinger

It's Halloween, and Carrie and I bypass the haunted house. She says her body is haunted, and we can play hide and seek in it.

Her skin is very, very soft, like chow hair or Persian cat. When I stroke her, she speaks in a hollow, distant voice, sounding 3,000 miles away,

instead of close by where we are under the sea green comforter on her water bed.

"My body is haunted by a man who tried to rape me. My body is haunted by a man who did rape me. My body is haunted by images of this man, that man. I don't see movies anymore because my life is a movie: *Flashbacks*. Rated R."

Gliding my hands over Carrie's smooth curves, I draw half-moons around her breasts. But I know she does not feel me touching her. Rattled like a rattlesnake, she floats near the ceiling like a ghost before disappearing out the door.

My fingers tiptoe carefully over her body of ice,

ice that will not shatter. "I am not a criminal," I whisper. "I will not hurt you."

Underneath the ice, life flows, gently, like a stream.

Survivor

Ki Russell

I'm sick of being named
survivor which sounds
so intentional, like flint
and steel in my pocket, a knife
sharpened and sheathed,
a canteen filled before
the woods surrounded me.

Like I knew what I was doing,
like it wasn't just stumbling
from thicket to bramble
to muck to meadow and back.

And I'm over being named
victim like my fingers inked
the rings of the target swirled
on my back. Villains begin
as victims, and I'm not
committing myself
to a script.

I am more than my suffering,
but what am I without it
wrapped in sunset orange
around my shoulders,
begging hunters not
to shoot as I shuffle
these woods on a path
that straddles return and joining
the breeze drifting the treetops?

Un-Becoming

Holly Spencer

I don't remember how it started, but it never took much. I covered my ears and buried my face in the pillow. They brought their fight into my room like erupting volcanoes, spitting out fear, blood and bruises like molten lava. Then, my dad smashed my mom on the nose, in that critical place most people call "the bridge," located between the eyes. He didn't blind her, but he thinned her optic nerve. She sees in grayscale. Any accidental hit to the face could rupture her remaining vision. I used to contemplate that fact in my young mind. I worried that some random thing would fall on my mom's nose hard enough to separate her retina and make her blind. Accidental, like a fist. It was a reasoned fear. An epic fear. A child's fear. I was six years old.

"Look at your cunt-mother."

I couldn't look up. Terror held my face down on the pillow, moist from warm breath and tears. My hands held the pillow's ends curled around my ears to block out his voice. I didn't know what a *cunt* was. This new "cunt" word was ugly and I didn't want to know one.

He told me that if I didn't look at her, I would

get spanked. I looked up from the pillow, my long hair matted to my cheeks, and then hurriedly put my face back down, but not before I saw the *cunt.* She was standing beyond the bed. She had no shirt on. He had ripped it off when she tried to get away from him. She stood there, bare, crying and bleeding, her giant, D-cup breasts streaked with blood as it flowed from her nose and down her chest in thick, red lines.

I passed out.

The next day, my father patted his lap for me to sit with him. I knew that the prior evening's events was an offense, a violence so wrong, but I couldn't fully reconcile my mom's leaking and bruised eyes to my father's fists. I knew he had done it because I saw it. I knew where her pain came from, but when he patted his lap for me to sit and play, I knew only my dad's insistent love for me, and I didn't hesitate. I didn't have a word for what had happened the night before. Later on, the words Domestic Abuse, with capital letters, made their way into my vocabulary, but that was a long way from that day.

I sat on dad's lap with my Snoopy and made up superhero scenes full of action and dialogue. Mom's eyes were purple and engorged, swollen to the point of cracking, but the two of them talked in easy tones.

I bounced Snoopy on his outstretched legs. I tilted Snoopy's black, plush snoot down on my dad's jeans and made sniffing sounds. He laughed. It pleased me that he laughed at my playing. I had no form, no reference, and no experience. There was only the 'now,' and I was playing, and they were talking, and it was like the night before had never happened. Except when I looked at her face, I would remember the rivulets of blood flowing down her breasts.

My mom kept dabbing her eyes where the blood seeped through the cracks in her swollen flesh saying things like, "She plays so well by herself, doesn't she, Gary?"

He chain-smoked Kools, careful not to look at her face, and agreed.

She waited until he fell asleep, his Kool in his right hand, hanging over the armrest of the couch. The ash was extended, crooked, and she took the green marble ashtray and put it underneath his hand to catch it. Then she tapped the filter on the cigarette lightly until it fell from between his fingers. She picked us up off his lap, my Snoopy and me. She took me in to the kitchen where my boots were waiting. I kept looking at her eyes, her bruised and seeping eyes. She saw me looking and smiled at me. "Shhhh. We just have to be quiet," she whispered.

She stuck my tassel cap on my head, careful to tuck my dirty-blonde hair underneath. She took me by my gloved hand and opened the kitchen door. We snuck out, quiet, but the wind grabbed the door and slammed it.

I looked back at the pressed snow leaving a map of our escape route. We were already through the backyard, near the end of the alley, when my father pushed open the kitchen door and came out onto the back porch.

I could smell my mother's hair as she pulled me

along. She smelled of the straightforward scent of Flex shampoo, no aloes, no oils, just clean. My tassel cap bobbed in the cold air and kept time as my boots mashed the snow. My short legs jogged to keep up with my mom's fast, even gait. My dad screamed my name, his voice thick, wounded.

I turned back when I heard him call out my name. My dad! I reached for him. She grabbed me under the arm with her other hand and then I was swinging upwards into the air. She caught me underneath the knees and cradled me as she jogged to the bus stop. We heard the phlegm-y sound of airbrakes that means a bus is near to braking and this made her jog a little faster. He screamed my name again. I struggled against her. I kicked my feet and cried.

I reached for him; I reached past my mother, with hands born of love, DNA, shared dimples and brown eyes. As I got older, I reassembled the memory of that night to fit my snotty disdain for the victim, my mother. I looked down at her as if I were better than her because I was too smart, too reasoned, and too tough to let that happen to me. It was a conflict that should not have existed: How dare she let him hurt her versus it wasn't his fault. I reached inside myself and twisted the memory, forcing the pieces to fit in the defense of my father, and when it was all said and done, I found myself involved with tyrants who called violence passion and whose apologies always placed the blame on me.

I kept reaching well into my thirties, past a ruptured-spleen, blood-filled lungs, a broken pelvis, and an eternity of black eyes and bruises that connect the dots on the Male Relationship Timeline of my life with red Sharpie, red as blood. I've been opened up and drained, emptied, sewn back together, bandaged by doctors and therapists and with a denial so thick and cool, it laid like a salve over my wounds.

I kept reaching until the last blow felt more like synchronicity than fate, blood coursing down my chest in great red rivers over the small B-cups of my breasts, and I realized I had become the *cunt.* I had become a *cunt* because a *cunt* bleeds and is meant to bleed. A *cunt* gets beaten and broken. A *cunt* equals blood streaming down her breasts, because it's always a "her," and if he said she was a *cunt* and you saw the *cunt*, then she had to be a *cunt.* It seemed fitting that this was the way I would begin and un-become, running towards a different bus at a different bus stop separated not by city miles but by years, my hand flagging it down, reaching for it.

Today, I remember the child who hid her face in a pillow, who passed out to not see anymore, whose first moment of heartbreak, rended between her love for the one who hit and the one who got hit, grew from a nasty word meant to demean and strip bare, and finally metastasized into a volcano of her own, covering everything with plumes of noxious blood and ash, making the land uninhabitable.

I understand that these moments are why people get drunk, shoot dope, jump out of airplanes, gamble their rent money; this is why people chase and cling to other people, make shallow cuts along their legs and arms, eat a gallon of chocolate ice cream on the couch while binge-watching serial television, horde magazines and books and dishes and clothes until they bury the heartache beneath the excess.

On that day, forty years ago, my mother and I saw the bus at the same time, and while she reached for it, reached for her own un-becoming, and let me see it could be done, my tassel cap bobbed up and down.

I Am Disheartened

Bonnie Brady

I am disheartened. A young woman in my town (but it could have been any one of hundreds of towns) had her life taken by another enraged man who thought…what? That because she had once said yes, she had relinquished her right to say no? That if he couldn't have her, nobody could have her? That she was his property? That her poor choices warranted the death penalty? That if he waved a gun around she would change her mind and love him?

I can't abide this toxic masculinity. Those hormone fueled urges that only know how to destroy the object of attention, that cannot turn and walk away, that cannot grasp the concept of "enough." I am disheartened that all the "good guys" out there, who would not harass, or stalk, or assault, or wield their power or physical strength to control a woman, also stand by and fail to intervene when they see the misogyny of a friend, co-worker, family member, or just some guy in a bar, or a parking lot, or a locker room talking trash or behaving badly toward a woman.

The evening after the young woman was

murdered, I came out of a restaurant and, as I stood on the walkway facing the highway, a car passed by. There were four young men hanging out of the windows yelling, "We want some pussy! We want some pussy!" They were yelling and laughing and generally making asses of themselves. I'm an old lady and I doubt they were yelling at me, but it deeply offended and saddened me. How has this behavior become okay? And what is the path that starts with young men somehow feeling entitled to "some pussy" and leads to a young woman being shot numerous times point blank by an enraged former lover?

What failure to evolve has rendered so many boys and men to feel it's their privilege to figuratively drag a girl off to their cave by the hair?

When I was about twelve years old, I was riding my bike around my neighborhood in Los Angeles. It was a nice neighborhood; I had always felt safe there. As I rode by, a man sitting in his parked car raised up his hips and exposed his enormous erect penis to me. I rode past as fast as I could and made a beeline for home. That was when I first realized that men were dangerous.

How is a young girl supposed to navigate in this milieu? What can she wear that isn't found provocative by someone, somewhere? How much make-up is enough? Too much, cheap, trashy? How can she know if a friend request on Facebook is just a kid her own age who wants lots of "virtual" friends, or a forty-year-old sexual predator? And how can she learn to make good choices when the learning curve holds so many risks? When a poor choice isn't just a valuable, if tough, learning experience., but can result in life-threatening injury, sexual assault, emotional trauma, or even death.

I am disheartened. I feel hopeless. I have no answers and I don't know anyone who does. But I'm tired of women having to defend themselves from what is essentially a men's problem. It's time for men to collectively step up and deal with their own shit. Figure it out. Evolve, already!

Elegy for Sally and Rose

Alderson Women's Prison, West Virginia

Christina Lovin

Speak to me sisters, as we pass
    in the yard.
Speak to me in the words of freedom,
of liberty as you saw it. Look me
    in the eye
and tell me it was worth it, whatever
    it was—
an ideal, a man, a roof overhead
    and a meal.

Remember the power your voices held,
    how men
would listen when you spoke,
    your mouths warm
with seditious honey, your tongues
    fascinating
as serpents' forks with the lies
    they feared.
But every man adores a spy—
    his mother
asking questions of the stained
    handkerchief,

his little woman watching the clock
  till dawn,
waiting for the whiskey breath
  and alibi.
What woman would not want
  to be you?

And what woman could not fear
  you, safe
in her house-dressed world,
  considering you,
dangerous in numbered khaki?
  Remember,
we are all at the work of women
  on their hands
and knees, scrubbing the dirt of life
  from a floor
we have not soiled, wiping away
  the wet stains
of sex from our bodies and beds.
  It is woman's
place, you know, to sow where she will
  not reap,
sew the things she will not wear,
  and be thankful

to clean up the mess afterward.
  A jury of your
true peers—trusting women, misled,
  led on,
turned down, knocked up, abused,
  and abandoned—
would have found you guilty as traitors

to no one
but yourselves. Caged, a lark refuses
to sing
but a few broken chords remembered
from her
freedom. Sing, my sisters, sing.
You are us.
We hear your voices echoing
through the tunnel,
reverberating from the cell block
to solitary.

Taking Tongues

Sarah Fawn Montgomery

Today I take tongues
from the mouths of men
like ears soldiers stole
from the dead during wars
we could not wage because
of breasts and the good
sense of our fairer sex.
To be fair, I will not ask
permission either, pluck
prizes to dangle at my throat,
grotesque and spectacular.

I'm taking tongues to task
for what I'm forbidden
to say: the times I fucked
boys, girls to gasping,
claimed my portion of the bread
basket and subway seat,
finished my sentence
uninterrupted, did not apologize
or *smile sweetie*, convinced doctors
my pain was real, my boss
not to cup my knee

while correcting me. I'll insist
the neighbor a terrible guitarist
no matter how he croons
at me while his wife is away,
and voice artillery at catcallers
with their canary whistles.

Soldiers brought ears home
to hear stories of their glories:
I'm taking tongues to tell of mine.

Rebirth is a Mother

Kari Nguyen

If she pushes her arms up, the boards above her will move and there will be light. If she pushes her arms up, the dirt over the boards will loosen and there will be light. If she pushes her arms up and lets the light in she will also let in the air, but if she uses both arms to push, as she must, as she has tried doing so with just the left hand and then the right, alternately, then she must first lower her baby, which she has come to call Mine, onto the ground, and from standing in this dark place she knows there is something moving quietly and occasionally and furtively near her legs. Someone told her, hours, days, or years ago—who really could tell?—that it was better down here. That once they lowered you, they could no longer touch you. But the sounds up there have stopped—there had been explosions nearby—and the air would be gone soon if she didn't try. She knew there were roots exposed here; she had felt them. She spread her legs as wide as she could, achingly wide—could she reach both sides of the hole? Could she shimmy her legs up the sides like Jackie Chan? Could she loosen a root with her foot and break it free? Could she sharpen it with the heel of her shoe, or with her teeth? Could she hold Mine in one arm, and shimmy her legs up the sides, up up, holding the sharpened root in her teeth, using her free arm and her head and the straining muscles of her neck to push past the boards, keeping Mine's head pressed against her chest, and would her legs, already shaking so badly, would they support them both long enough to get an elbow and then a knee, then her belly up, the root by now in her free hand. She would roll along the ground, sheltering Mine and the weaponized root, given over from a tree or a shrub no longer needing water to survive, no longer needing anything, just giving this last gift. There would be no explosions, or if there were, Mother of Mine would avoid them, rolling past the fires, mother and child and tree; they would roll around them and sweep up the others they found, dirt-streaked, no-haired, full-haired, clothed or not clothed, they would gather all of them, a large mass of rolling roots with sharp points, rolling and collecting and protecting, on and on, as large as a planet, and finally, the planet would slow and eventually come to a stop, and then it would begin to rise, and tilt, and spin, loosening dirt and root and flesh and pebble and warmth and sound and every child—every last one of them—would come shooting out, laughing, spinning, tumbling head over heels to land softly all over the world while their mothers held hands in the sky and rained down their tears of joy.

The Antlered Woman Responds

After Mark Doty

Ki Russell

On misty-gray, not-dark, not-light days
I feel bone sprout from my temples.
I try to catch a glimpse in store windows.

I should keep my eyes on the ground
instead of stepping out of forwardness.
But my allegiance is not to permanent forms.

Plain clothes hide hooves and haunches,
the elongated grammar of muscle,
and me without a trench coat.

I am the respiration of the grass
and my animal alphabet
fails on a regular basis.

Years from now on a tonal night
my feet will evaporate into cloud
and my antlers will twine with stardust.

For now I am less anatomy
than a storm, a glittering, gathering mass,
an antlered woman dodging traffic.

How to Become Baba Yaga

Ki Russell

Build a log hut and stuff
the cracks with mud, straw,
rags. Twine hair through dirt.
Decorate with skulls.
Sculpt a pair of chicken legs
from river clay and rooster
blood. Place them beneath the floor.
Rig ropes with winches and puppet
your home wherever you please.
Compose chants and curses.
Mumble them as you tug tendons.

Pull your nose to your chin.
Pinch veins until the skin blues
and people miss your eyes.
Hunch your shoulders
in a hill that slopes
to your head. Oil
your hair till it snakes
around your face. Knock out
every other tooth and sharpen
the rest. You'll need them
to tear flesh from bones.

Train your palate:
melt flesh on your tongue.
Savor the juice of roast
torso, mop the drippings
with bone-flour bread. Lick
your fingers clean. Pluck lips
from your teeth. Devour
their sins. Gulp
them down. Absolve.

Litany of Collective Cuntsciousness

Susan Abbott
4 July 2018

We cannot fight old power in old power terms only. The only way we can do it is by creating another whole structure that touches every aspect of our experience at the same time as we are resisting. —Audre Lorde

In the beginning was the word
and that word was
CUNT*
moves across the face of the deep cunt
we are wondrously made cunt
from the splendor of the morning light cunt
flow these wishes for the common good cunt.

Out of the cradle endlessly rocking cunt
I hear America singing cunt
o beautiful for spacious sky cunt
land of milk and honey cunt
huddled masses yearning to breathe free cunt
music of those who have walked out of slavery cunt
we who believe in freedom shall not rest cunt
lift every voice and sing cunt
till earth and heaven ring cunt

teach your children well cunt
emancipate yourself from mental slavery cunt
only ourselves can free our mind cunt
redemption cunt.

Breathe in experience cunt
breathe out poetry cunt
wars I have seen cunt
a woman is talking to death cunt
dream of a common language cunt
a room of one's own cunt
a rose is a rose cunt
lifting belly cunt
as a wife has a cow cunt
the clitoris in her least speech cunt
let freedom ring cunt.

Ancestral cunt, cosmic cunt
ultimate cunt, verbatim cunt
coherent cunt, deterrent cunt
universal cunt, particular cunt
paraded cunt, blockaded cunt
truncated cunt, circuitous cunt
spell-binding cunt, fact-finding cunt
spooning cunt, ballooning cunt
feckless cunt, reckless cunt
sensational cunt, relational cunt
informational cunt, confrontational cunt
mind-your-own-beeswax cunt.

Glamorous cunt, polyamorous cunt
candid cunt, splendid cunt
mountain-moving cunt, loudmouth cunt

missing cunt, kissing cunt
big woman things cunt
old woman springs cunt
leads me to lie down in green meadows cunt
restores my soul cunt
full of grace cunt
in your face cunt
ship in the harbor cunt
mother and child cunt
hold you awhile cunt
how could anyone ever tell you cunt
you are anything less than beautiful cunt
how deeply you're connected to my soul cunt.

Alpha cunt, omega cunt
end-of-story cunt
never again cunt
always and forever cunt
fat lady singing cunt.

*CUNT: v. a process and function of the imagination whereby ideas and flashes of insight/ creativity are fleshed out and given the life they deserve; n. an idea, spirit, deva, the soul seed of joy, peace, harmony and well-being embedded in every fiber in existence; adj. a causative factor in some instances of apoplexy and spontaneous human combustion.

Outspoken

Sarah Fawn Montgomery

Once upon some time
a woman laughed and pearls fell
from her lips, luminescent
like her teeth and the moon,
roses, too, dropping like syllables.
Another town and time
a woman shouted and darts
launched from her throat,
enunciation precise and glinting.

I want to be the woman
who casts creeping vines
with my words, leaves
unfurling, spreading shadow,
sends moths from my mouth,
wings beating iambic,
bright eyespots blinking
at the dumbstruck world.

About the Contributors

Susan Abbott writes and paints from her perch in the shadow of Mt. San Jacinto in Desert Hot Springs, CA. Her work has appeared in *Cholla Needles, Mago Journal, Awakenings, So's Your Old Lady, Sojourner*, and *Between Ourselves: Letters between Mothers and Daughters.* Her chapbook *Nasty Woman Rise* was published by Cholla Needles in 2017. Check out her art work at Susan Abbott Watercolors on Facebook and @smtabbott on Instagram.

Liz Abrams-Morley's newest collection, *Beholder*, was published by Word Poetry. *Inventory* was published by Finishing Line Press. *Necessary Turns* was published by Word Press and won an Eric Hoffer Book Award. Her poems and short stories have been published in a variety of anthologies, journals, and ezines and have been read on NPR. She is co-founder of Around the Block Writing Collaborative (aroundtheblockwriters.org). A professor at Rosemont's MFA program who also teaches children at all levels in literacy, Liz is an activist, wife, mother, grandma, and sister. lizabramsmorley.com

Lisa Allen's work has appeared or is forthcoming in the anthology *Listen to Your Mother* (G.P. Putnam's Sons), *Unmasking: Solstice MFA Anthology*, and *Bacopa Literary Review.* Lisa holds an MFA from The Solstice Low-Residency MFA in Creative Writing Program at Pine Manor College, where she was awarded a Michael Steinberg Fellowship for Creative Nonfiction.

Dori Appel's poems have been widely published in magazines and anthologies, as well as in her collection of poems, *Another Rude Awakening* (Cherry Grove Collections). A playwright as well as a poet, she is the author of many published plays and monologues and was the winner of the Oregon Book Award in Drama in 1998, 1999, and 2001. She lives and writes in Ashland, Oregon. doriappel.com.

Judith Arcana writes poems, stories, essays, and books and hosts a poetry show on KBOO in Oregon. Recently, *Announcements from the Planetarium* was published by Flowstone Press, and Eberhardt Press brought out a new edition of *4th Period English*. Visit juditharcana.com for more information.

Tina Barry's writing appears in numerous anthologies and literary publications including *Nasty Women Poets: An Unapologetic Anthology of Subversive Verse*, *The Best Short Fiction 2016*, and *Drunken Boat*. She is the author of *Mall Flower* (Big Table Publishing). Find her at TinaBarryWriter.com.

Bonnie Brady graduated from USC in the middle ages and is a retired Occupational Therapist, late-blooming artist, and writer. She lives in Yucca Valley, CA, with her husband Paul, 5 dogs, a cat, 4 ducks, and 2 hens.

Gayle Brandeis is the author of the memoir *The Art of Misdiagnosis: Surviving My Mother's Suicide* (Beacon Press), the poetry collection, *The Selfless Bliss of the Body* (Finishing Line Press), the craft book, *Fruitflesh: Seeds of Inspiration for Women Who Write* (HarperOne), and several novels. She teaches at Sierra Nevada College and Antioch University Los Angeles.

Marion Deutsche Cohen is the author of 26 collections of poetry or memoir; her latest poetry collection is *New Heights in Non-Structure* (dancing girl press, about home-schooling and other ideas about engaging with children). She is also the author of two controversial memoirs about spousal chronic illness, a trilogy diary of late-pregnancy loss, and *Crossing the Equal Sign* (Plain View Press, about the experience of mathematics). She teaches math and writing at Arcadia University in Glenside, PA. marioncohen.net.

Kym Cunningham received her MFA from San Jose State University with emphases in creative nonfiction and poetry. She acted as the lead Nonfiction Editor of Reed Magazine, the oldest literary magazine west of the Mississippi. She received the Ida Fay Sachs Ludwig Memorial Scholarship, the Academy of American Poets Prize, MARY's Editor's Prize, and two Pushcart Prize nominations. Her writing has been published in more than a dozen literary journals and two anthologies. Her first poetry chapbook was published in February 2018.

Caryn Davidson is the education coordinator at Big Morongo Canyon Preserve. She retired from Joshua Tree National Park in 2017. Caryn holds a master's degree in French from UCLA and worked for the French consulate in Los Angeles. Her work has been published in *L.A. Weekly, LAICA Journal, The Stone, Pacific Crest Trailside Reader, GEO, Spillway, Phantom Seed,* and *Luna Arcana.*

Holly E. Dunlap is a writing instructor at Auburn University, an MFA student at Vermont College of Fine Arts, and published her first full-length book of poetry in 2015. Holly is a single mother, poet, and writing instructor. She mucks through life, finding bits of mica and other shiny things. Also, sometimes she enjoys arranging toys in her daughter's playroom, pretending she's cleaning. The outdoors and animals are her friends, but she's allergic to them all. Still, she explores with her daughter.

Sarah Einstein lives, writes, and teaches in Chattanooga, TN. She is the author of *Mot: A Memoir* (University of Georgia Press) and *Remnants of Passion* (SheBooks), and her work has been awarded a Pushcart, a Best of the Net, and the AWP Prize in Creative Nonfiction.

Alexis Rhone Fancher's books include: *How I Lost My Virginity to Michael Cohen and other heart-stab poems* (Sybaritic Press), *State of Grace: The Joshua Elegies* (KYSO Flash), *Enter Here* (KYSO Flash), *and Junkie Wife* (Moontide Press). She is published in *Best American Poetry 2016, Rattle, Hobart, Verse Daily, Plume, Tinderbox*, and elsewhere. A multiple Pushcart Prize nominee, Alexis is poetry editor of *Cultural Weekly*. alexisrhonefancher.com

Ann Marie Gamble is an editor at an advertising agency in the Midwest. She writes fiction as well as poetry, and practices keeping it pithy on Twitter.

Tania Hammidi is a performer, educator, and arts organizer living in Joshua Tree, CA. Hammidi is the director of Dapper Dates Shop (@dapperdates246), a food justice game and farmer's market booth, aimed at sharing the farming history and health benefits of organic dates of the Mojave desert. Hammidi also hosts *Queer Salon, Joshua Tree*, a monthly arts and eating salon for Mojave desert LGBTQIAA+ folk and friends. Hammidi earned a Ph.D. in Critical Dance Studies from U.C. Riverside (2011) and an M.S. in Community Development from U.C. Davis (1999).

Hanan Hazime is a poet, a story teller, and a scripturient wordsmith living in Toronto. She has a Master of Arts degree in English Literature and Creative Writing from the University of Windsor. She is the 2017-2018 Writer in Residence and Literary Arts Instructor at Workman Arts.

Alice Kaltman is the author of the story collection *Staggerwing* (Tortoise Books) and the novel *Wavehouse* (Fitzroy Books). Her stories appear in numerous journals including *Hobart, WhiskeyPaper, Joyland*, and *BULL: Men's Fiction*, and in the anthologies *The Pleasure You Suffer* (Tortoise Books) and *On Montauk* (Harbor Electronic Publishing). Alice lives, writes and surfs in Brooklyn and Montauk, New York.

Genevieve Kersten is a writer and professional semi-finalist. Her poetry has appeared in *Helen: a literary magazine* and *Here Comes Everyone*. She is the poetry editor for *Okay Donkey*. Find her on twitter @genekresten or @okaydonkeymag.

Christina Lovin's writing has appeared in over one hundred different literary journals and anthologies, as well as five volumes of poetry: *Echo* (Bottom Dog

Press), *A Stirring in the Dark* (Old Seventy Creek Press), *Flesh* (Finishing Line Press), *Little Fires* (Finishing Line Press), and *What We Burned for Warmth* (Finishing Line Press). She has received writing grants from Kentucky Arts Council, Kentucky Foundation for Women, and the Elizabeth George Foundation.

Fiction, nonfiction, and experimental prose writer **Jana Martin** is the author of *Russian Lover and Other Stories* (Verse Chorus Press) and is a contributing editor to TheWeeklings.com. She has appeared in *Glimmer Train, the Mississippi Review, Five Points, The Village Voice, The New York Times, Tinker Street, Post Road,* and in the forthcoming anthology *Women Who Rock* (Black Dog & Leventhal). She was recently the writer in residence at SUNY New Paltz. She lives, writes, and edits in the Hudson Valley.

Sarah Fawn Montgomery is the author of *Quite Mad: An American Pharma Memoir* (Ohio State University Press) and the poetry chapbooks *Regenerate: Poems from Mad Women* (dancing girl press), *Leaving Tracks: A Prairie Guide* (Finishing Line Press), and *The Astronaut Checks His Watch* (Finishing Line Press). She has been *Prairie Schooner*'s Nonfiction Editor since 2011 and is Assistant Professor at Bridgewater State University.

Brenda Morisse is a poet. She loves her children and her dog, Bella. She hates trump. She loves being a feminist and living in the Bronx. She hates trump. She loves equal rights and kindness but ever since the trump installation, her psyche has been in a panic. She hates bigotry and misogyny and racism and cruelty to children and animals. She hates trump. She hates trump and his policy of kidnapping children and incarcerating babies. She hates trump.

Kari Nguyen's fiction and nonfiction appear online and in print, including in the following books: *The Best of Boston Literary Magazine Volume One* and *The Exquisite Quartet Anthology 2012*. Kari is the former nonfiction editor for *Stymie Magazine* and curator of *Stymie*'s "Why I Write" column. Find her at karinguyen.wordpress.com.

Devon Ortega obtained a bachelor's degree from The Ohio State University and a master's degree from Ohio University. She currently lives in Pickerington, Ohio, with her husband and four children.

Ailey O'Toole is a queer poet and bartender who writes about feminism, empathy, and pain. Her work has previously appeared in or is forthcoming from *After the Pause, Ghost City Review, Rising Phoenix Review, Okay Donkey*, and others. She tweets at @ms_ocoole.

Alzenira Quezada is a Maestra Vocalista and Writer with a Master of Fine Art from Stonecoast MFA in Portland, Maine. They are an internationally known performance artist, published author of lyric fusion poetry, photographer, and art director, who is currently collaborating on works in Mexico.

Tracy Robert is a member of the resistance and hosts a local huddle in southern California. Her book of linked novellas, *Flashcards and The Curse of Ambrosia* (2015), won the Many Voices Project prize at New Rivers Press.

Ki Russell is author of *The Wolf at the Door* (Ars Omnia Publishing), *Antler Woman Responds* (Paladin Contemporaries), and *How to Become Baba Yaga* (Medulla Publishing). She is a contributing editor for *Phantom Drift: a Journal of New Fabulism* and a peer reviewer for *Whale Road Review.*

Janette Schafer is a freelance writer, nature photographer, part-time rocker, and full-time banker living in Pittsburgh, Pennsylvania. Recent publications of her writing and photographs include: *New Ink; Armarolla; PublicSource; Eunoia Review; Rigorous Journal.* Her play, Mad Virginia, has been selected for this year's Pittsburgh Original Short Play Series in July 2018. Janette will begin her MFA studies in Creative Writing at Chatham University this fall.

Eva Schlesinger is a two-time Moth StorySLAM champion, whose performances also include "Talk Amongst Yourselves: An Evening of Jew Dyke Performance," where she presented "Halloween," the Herstories Project, and Poets Against Rape. Her writing has appeared in *Hashtag Queer, Riggwelter, former cactus, Tattoo Highway*, and *Women in Clothes.*

Nina Shengold wrote the novel *Clearcut* (Random House) and *River of Words: Portraits of Hudson Valley Writers*, with photographer Jennifer May (SUNY Press). She won a Writers Guild Award for her teleplay *Labor of Love* and an ABC Playwright Award for *Homesteaders.* She lives in the feckless Catskills.

Holly Spencer is a native Pittsburgher where she lives with her three dogs and two cats. Her work has appeared in *Jet Fuel Review, Anti-Heroin Chic, Rise Up Review,* and *Pink Panther Magazine.* She will be attending Chatham University as an MFA grad student in the fall of 2018 as an awardee of the Words Without Walls Fellowship.

Alison Stone has published five full-length collections, *Dazzle* (Jacar Press), *Masterplan* (with Eric Greinke, Presa Press), *Ordinary Magic,* (NYQ Books), *Dangerous Enough* (Presa Press), and *They Sing at Midnight,* which won the 2003 Many Mountains Moving Poetry Award; as well as three chapbooks. Her poems have appeared in *The Paris Review, Poetry, Ploughshares, Barrow Street, Poet Lore,* and elsewhere. She has been awarded *Poetry*'s Frederick Bock Prize and *New York Quarterly*'s Madeline Sadin Award. stonepoetry.org.

Donna Jo Thorndale is a Los Angeles-based actress and writer. Originally from Kentucky, she lives in a Spanish Bungalow with her exquisite pit bull, Juliet Capulet, and two Meyer lemon trees. She is writing about food, politics, dogs, and meditation.

Keri Withington is an Appalachian based poet whose work has previously appeared in numerous journals and anthologies, recently including *Blue Fifth Review, Tittynope Zine,* and *The Wild Word.* Her first chapbook, *Constellation of Freckles,* is forthcoming from Dancing Girl Press. She is an assistant professor of English at Pellissippi State.

About the Editor

Susan Rukeyser wrote the novel, *Not On Fire, Only Dying* (Twisted Road Publications, 2015), an SPD Fiction Bestseller and a finalist for the 2016 Lascaux Prize for published books. Her flash fiction chapbook, *Swap / Meet* (Space Cowboy Books, 2018), is a loosely-linked collection inspired by classified ads. Susan's work appears in a number of journals including *Hippocampus Magazine*, *Atticus Review*, *WhiskeyPaper*, *Monkeybicycle*, and *Women Writers, Women's Books*. She is the former Reviews Editor for *Necessary Fiction*. In 2017 she moved home to the Mojave although she grew up in Connecticut.

Find her here: susanrukeyser.com.

Editor's Acknowledgements

I might not have attempted this book if Richard Soos, poet and publisher of Cholla Needles, had not been so sure I could do it. Generous with his time and advice, his reassuring demeanor kept me on track. Artist and poet Susan Abbott was an indispensable part of this project, as both contributor and editorial consultant, sharing her deep understanding of feminist theory and the modern women's movement. As ever, I relied on Ed White. He answered endless questions about publishing, distribution, terms, and publicity. Author Jean-Paul L. Garnier, co-owner of Space Cowboy Books, which published my chapbook, *Swap / Meet*, helped me understand the many factors to consider with book design. Mia Torres offered unconditional support of this book and me, providing feedback and encouragement when doubt crept in. Much gratitude, also, to my online writers' community. I don't know how I would have survived the 2016 campaign season without you. We shared art and words and fury. I said yes to this book because I knew you were out there, raising your voices in protest, your tender hearts broken. Better days are coming. Until then: dare.

27099498R00095

Made in the USA
Columbia, SC
18 September 2018